THE PUBLIC LIVES OF RURAL OLDER AMERICANS

Steven A. Peterson
Robert J. Maiden

UNIVERSITY
PRESS OF
AMERICA

Lanham • New York • London

Library of Congress Cataloging-in-Publication Data

Peterson, Steven A.
The public lives of rural older Americans / Steven A. Peterson,
Robert J. Maiden.
p.   cm.
1. Rural aged—United States—Case studies.   2. United States—
Rural conditions—Case studies.   I. Maiden, Robert J.   II. Title.
HQ1064.U5P483   1993
305.26'0973—dc20   93–13840 CIP

ISBN 0–8191–9188–4 (cloth : alk. paper)
ISBN 0–8191–9189–2 (pbk. : alk. paper)

To Bettina Franzese and Evan Franzese-Peterson and to Patricia Maiden and Robert Maiden, James Maiden, Michael Maiden, and Francesca Maiden—our spouses and children whose love, personal sacrifices, and advice sustained and guided us throughout this research project

Contents

Preface

This book represents the culmination of nearly a decade of work in which we have focused upon the elderly in Allegany County, New York. In this period of time, we have analyzed and reanalyzed our data many different times. We have come to believe that the elderly in this rural, upstate county can tell us something about the public lives of those Americans similarly situated throughout the country.

Ours, of course, is a case study. We cannot pretend that the people with whom we have become so familiar in this one county truly represent rural elderly elsewhere. External validity remains an issue. However, we do believe that this one in-depth examination complements other volumes that take a more global view of rural elderly. In that sense, we provide an idiographic component to the several more general nomothetic works on the subject.

Acknowledgements are in order. We must thank Elizabeth Embser-Wattenberg, the former Director of the Allegany County Office for the Aging, for the great support that she provided us in both the 1983 and the 1987 surveys. Without her efforts, we probably never would have undertaken this project.

We also acknowledge financial support provided by the New York State Office of Aging for the 1983 survey. In 1987, we received support from a number of organizations to carry out the interviews. In particular, we thank ACCORD, the Jones Memorial Hospital, St. James Mercy Hospital, Jan & Bev's Nursing Service, the Allegany County Office for the Aging, and the Alfred Housing Corporation.

Finally, we want to acknowledge—with gratitude—some very special people who provided moral and emotional support, in particular Bettina Franzese and Evan Franzese-Peterson and Patricia Maiden and Reba Gleason.

Chapter 1

Introduction

Introduction

Rural aging is an understudied area. Two recent books have explored rural aging, John Krout's *The Aged in Rural America* (1986) and Raymond Coward and Gary Bell's *The Elderly in Rural America* (1985). A sizable number of journal publications have appeared, too. Nonetheless, more depth in the research base is called for. The two books noted above make major contributions to the field of rural aging and provide a wealth of much needed information about the important dimensions and factors affecting the aging processes in the context of rural America. However, they tend to present a broad sweeping view of the rural aged. The volumes focus on demographic patterns and cite a large array of studies that include many urban comparisons. While this information is important and fills a gap, the field of rural aging also requires a focused in-depth case study. An analysis of one rural county in detail examines the particular in order to flesh out the general patterns. The latter is the focus of this volume. In grander terms, ours is an idiographic study that grounds the more general research in very concrete specifics.

Furthermore, many of the authors' definitions of "rural" are quite broad, as they straightforwardly note. For example, they cite many articles drawing data from counties that contained small urban cities (populations up to 50,000). Because of these larger population bases, it is frequently difficult to understand what kinds of rural and urban comparisons are being made.

Thus, we believe that the picture of rural life thus rendered is incomplete. We present an in-depth case study of one quintessential rural county in western New York to fill the gap. Allegany County is a

1

good choice for a case study for many reasons. It exemplifies the many similar rural and sparsely populated counties throughout America. Kim notes that (1983: 105) "Of the nation's 3,135 counties, 2,210 (70 percent) have fewer than 50,000 persons. . . ." Thus, much of America is rural.

Allegany County, like many rural counties, has a substantial elderly population. Younger generations tend to migrate to urban areas seeking their fame and fortune, often leaving their parents and grandparents behind. And, like many rural counties, it is impoverished and resource poor compared to resource rich urban counties. Many of the elderly in Allegany County live in poverty. They, in turn, frequently lack social services and other resources necessary to sustain an adequate standard of living (not unusual in rural counties; see, e.g., Kim, 1983).

In our text, we examine the needs and concerns of the elderly in this county. We highlight **both** the basic everyday **and** the universal themes that underlie daily living in the area and, in general, that underlie living in rural America.

In advocating programs to help the elderly in rural communities, we need to have as accurate a portrayal of their quality of life as possible. We need to learn more about the important variables related to aging. We need this information extracted from broadly-based macro-ecological studies, like the ones mentioned above, as well as from more narrowly focused micro-anthropological studies, such as ours.

What does the title of our book refer to? By public lives, we mean the manner in which people daily interact with public agencies, government, and the world of politics. Most data in this volume come from in-depth face-to-face surveys conducted in Allegany County. This information is supplemented by general reviews of the rural aging literature and by reference to data from the National Opinion Research Center's (NORC) General Social Survey. This strengthens the conclusions that we arrive at using the case study approach.

Rural Elderly

What are characteristics of the rural elderly? There are several distinct dimensions where rural and nonrural elderly differ. Krout summarizes the standard viewpoint when he says that (1986: 7) ". . . it is . . . generally agreed that rural areas are characterized by greater poverty, less adequate housing and transportation, and a lack of availability and accessibility of a wide range of services when compared to urban places.'' While actual findings are not always quite so clearcut, this brief precis is a useful starting point (Generally, see Krout, 1986; Coward and Lee, 1985; *Old Age and Ruralism*, 1980).

Demographics. Cities are not as attractive to the elderly as they once might have been, although many of America's elderly still live in urban areas. The greatest, most rapid growth of the elderly has been in the suburbs. As Longino notes (1990: 50), ''. . . the most dramatic shifts since the 1950s have resulted in a rapidly growing suburban elderly population. Aging in place and net migration gains from central cities account for this trend.'' Longino also points out that (1990: 48) ''When their disabilities mount, the rural elderly often move to cities to be with their children.'' However, there are still many older Americans residing in rural areas.

About 26% of the American elderly live in rural areas (Meddin and Vaux, 1988; Golant, 1990). The old-old (75–84) and oldest-old are more likely to live outside metropolitan areas. Golant notes that (1990: 81) ''. . . by 1988 the elderly population was still more likely to occupy nonmetropolitan areas than the total population. . . .'' 26% of the elderly as opposed to 22.4% of the total population called rural America their home in 1988.

By 1988, the bulk of the elderly population lived in suburbs. The rural elderly were the least mobile as compared with urban and suburban elderly (Golant, 1987). Furthermore, rural elderly are more apt to migrate to warmer climates on merely a seasonal basis rather than a permanent basis, a pattern somewhat different from their urban and suburban peers (Steiness and Hogan, 1992).

Even though the rural elderly are not growing rapidly in number compared with their less rural cohorts, many rural elderly face problems that create important policy challenges to government. In many rural counties, for example, one in five citizens is 60 or older. The proportion of elderly in these communities is rising (particularly in the northeast and Midwest) and is expected to do so well into the future.

Quality of life. We know quite a bit about life satisfaction among the elderly in general. First, it is worth noting that Campbell, Converse, and Rodgers (1976) report that the young-old (65–74) and the old-old (75 and older) are the two age cohorts with the highest levels of life satisfaction. Among older Americans, the factors associated with greater life satisfaction are a sense that people are better off than relatives (Usui, Keil, and Durig, 1985), better health (Okun and Stock, 1987; Snow and Crapo, 1982), and emotional bondedness (Snow and

Crapo, 1982). Owning pets may make little difference (Lawton, Moss, and Moles, 1984). Research also indicates that life satisfaction is rather stable among older Americans (Baur and Okun, 1983); furthermore, and perhaps surprising to some, the same causal dynamics underlie life satisfaction between blacks and whites (Usui, Keil, and Phillips, 1983) and between males and females (Liang, 1982).

Living in rural areas is indirectly related to higher life satisfaction (Liang and Warfel, 1983), although there are no great differences between rural and nonrural elderly on this score (Krout, 1986; Speake and Cowart, 1988). Life satisfaction of rural elderly is very high, to begin with (Krout, 1986). Factors affecting greater sense of well-being include sense of mastery over the environment, low self-denigration, good health, not having experienced many negative life events (death of a spouse or having been a crime victim, for instance), and social support (Meddin and Vaux, 1988; Revicki and Mitchell, 1991). However, experts agree that much more remains to be learned (Scheidt, 1985; Lawton, 1985).

Economics of the rural elderly. Rural elderly tend to live in resource poor areas. One aspect of this is the so-called "dependency ratio," the percentage of elderly to those citizens in the "productive" years of 18 to 64. The ratio is larger in rural areas, indicating fewer tax-paying citizens for those who have for the most part retired. This puts some strain on the ability of such locales to provide services to the elderly (Krout, 1986). More to the point, rural elderly are generally poorer than their nonrural counterparts. A higher proportion live in poverty (Krout, 1986; *Old Age and . . .*, 1980).

Health. The rural elderly are more likely to rate their subjective health as poor or fair than their urban counterparts (Krout, 1986; Lassey and Lassey, 1985), although some studies suggest that the objective differences in health are not always very substantial (Krout, 1986, 1989). Poorer nutrition in rural elderly exacerbates health problems that they face (Glover, 1981). The standard view, in short, is that rural elders have greater health problems but get less care. Key barriers to receiving adequate health care are poverty, poor transportation, and reluctance of medical personnel to give complete care (Palmore, 1983). Access to health care, generally, is worse for rural and ghetto elderly (Kane and Kane, 1990).

With respect to mental health, rural elderly appear to be worse off than their peers (Wagonfeld, Goldsmith, Stiles, and Manderscheid, 1988). They face greater problems in terms of physical health, security, and loneliness (Kim, 1983), although depression may not differ much between urban and rural elderly (Hendricks and Turner, 1988). This is compounded by difficulties in delivering mental health services to rural elderly, among which problems are fewer health care facilities, low population density, less affluence, and fewer providers (Menolascino and Potter, 1989).

Housing. In rural areas, more elderly own their own homes—but their housing is of poorer quality than that utilized by their urban counterparts (Krout, 1986). A far larger proportion of rural homes lack complete plumbing facilities (Kim, 1983).

Transportation. Rural elderly face greater transportation problems. While a large percentage own their own cars, those who do not or who cannot drive often find themselves immobile, since well integrated public transportation systems are not normally available (Kim, 1983). Those who have the least mobility include females, those **not** owning cars, the unmarried or widowed, the less educated, elderly with physical mobility problems, and those without close neighborhood social ties (McGhee, 1983).

Nutrition. The standard view has it that rural elderly face more nutritional problems than nonrural elderly. Glover (1981) observes that rural elderly are a high risk group within an already nutritionally vulnerable population. Her reading of the evidence leads her to conclude that the quantity of food intake (calories) (1981: 102) ". . . may be a critical shortcoming of the diets of the rural elderly." Other research, though, clouds such straightforward conclusions (e.g., Lassey and Lassey, 1985; Krout, 1986; Norton and Wozny, 1984).

Services available to the elderly and their delivery. Previous paragraphs have already emphasized that there is often a shortage of services that rural elderly can call upon (and see Krout, 1986: 160–161). Others have commented upon the poor coordination of service delivery to the rural elderly (e.g., Ambrosius, 1981). However, some recent changes may be addressing this (e.g., Alter, 1988), as we discuss in our concluding chapter.

Rural Area Agencies on Aging (AAAs) have traditionally been deficient in terms of budget and staff resources needed to develop service delivery to the poor elderly and others in need (G. Nelson, 1980). Fewer services are available to rural elderly, as well. Rural elderly are less likely to participate in organizations generally; they are even less likely to take part in formal organizations, such as AARP (Kivett, 1985).

In fine, rural elderly have more problems, less access to services— but feel about as satisfied with their lives as those who are better off.

The 1987 National Opinion Research Center (NORC) General Social Survey (GSS) contains within it completed interviews with 359 Americans sixty years of age or older. Among questions asked of people were such basic demographic items as: marital status, number of group memberships, race, age, sex, education, and income. Table 1.1 reports upon how well these variables "predict" whether or not a respondent lives in a rural area, to see what differentiates rural residents from other older Americans. Betas from listwise multiple regression show that those living in rural areas are more apt to be married, to be white, to have less education, and lower incomes. This is one index of the proposition that those living in rural areas are distinct from those living elsewhere—thus justifying separating out this set of older Americans for further study.

Organization of Book

Chapter Two describes the two studies conducted in 1983 and 1987 in an upstate New York rural county. Characteristics of the samples are presented: these are compared with census data and with results from the NORC General Social Survey. They indicate that our samples are fairly typical of most rural elderly nationwide and represent well Allegany County's elderly.

Chapter Three begins by summarizing the existing literature on the nature and causes of rural older Americans' political behavior. Then, a more detailed analysis is carried out, using the case study data. The

Table 1.1. Multiple Regression: Predictors of Rural Residence, N = 306.

	Rural Residence
Married and never separated or never divorced	.17***
Number of group memberships	.07
Black	−.19****
Age	.07
Female	.00
Education	−.19***
Income	−.13*

* P < .10
** P < .05
*** P < .01
****P < .001

political behavior of the elderly is a topic of increasing importance as the elderly represent about 15% of our electorate and are more likely than any other age group to exercise their right to vote. The rural elderly are one important component of this larger group. We concentrate on the political orientations and behaviors of the rural elderly and on the constellation of factors affecting these. Specifically, we explore and underscore the impact that such important variables as health, life satisfaction and personality (such as extroversion, locus of control, neuroticism, and so on) have on the politics of the aged.

Many older Americans have contacts with programs designed to meet their unique needs. Chapter Four looks at the program encounters of the elderly. We explore past theories that explain what factors tend to influence the use or nonuse of social service programs, and we develop a multimodal theory explaining what factors lead to more program usage. Although the use of programs varied widely across our sample, program awareness was associated with usage. Therefore, we isolated both program awareness and program usage and examined the variables that were associated with each. We examine these questions—as well as why people contact bureaucracy about problems that they face.

Chapter Five examines the relationship between program use and two important sub-populations: the oldest-old (those over the age of 85) and women. We found that the oldest-old—the fastest growing segment of the population—had the greatest need for services although they were the least likely of any age group to receive them. Although women who live longer were most likely to fall into the oldest group, in general few gender differences of note were found. This information is important to policy makers and planners of social services as the numbers of oldest-old will continue to expand rapidly in the future.

Among the problems facing the elderly in rural America are social needs, housing, nutrition, and mental health. In Chapter Six, we examine these areas, using the model developed in Chapter Four as well as other theoretically relevant perspectives. This provides for more detailed understanding of the factors associated with need in different issue areas as well as those variables that shape program use. Results of these analyses are used to derive further policy suggestions.

The final chapter pulls together what has gone before. We present basic propositions supported by our different data sources; we specify policy implications of our conclusions. Finally, we speculate about the future in terms of rural older Americans' public lives.

In conclusion, our book focuses on an important subject. A substantial number of older Americans live in rural area. It is clear that certain problems loom larger for such residents, including transportation and gaining access to services. The elderly are an important part of the population of rural dwellers in the United States. And yet their public lives are relatively unknown. This book hopes to fill this gap in the research literature by portraying more thoroughly the nature of rural older Americans' contacts with public agencies and the essence of their political personal lives across many dimensions. We summarize much extant literature, and we report in much greater detail than heretofore the multifaceted components of their public lives.

References

Alter, Catherine Foster. 1988. The changing structure of elderly service delivery systems. *The Gerontologist* 28: 91–98.

Ambrosius, G. Richard. 1981. To dream the impossible dream—delivering coordinated services to the rural elderly. In Paul K. H. Kim and Constance P. Wilson (eds.), *Toward Mental Health of the Rural Elderly*. Washington, D. C.: University Press of America.

Baur, P. A. and M. A. Okun. 1983. Stability of life satisfaction in late life. *The Gerontologist* 23: 261–265.

Campbell, Angus, Philip E. Converse, and W. L. Rodgers 1976. *The Quality of American Life*. New York: Russell Sage Foundation.

Coward, Raymond and Raymond R. Bell. 1985. *The Elderly in Rural America*. New York: Springer.

Glover, Esther E. 1981. Nutrition and the rural elderly. In Paul K. H. Kim and Constance P. Wilson (eds.), *Toward Mental Health of the Rural Elderly*. Washington, D. C.: University Press of America.

Golant, Stephen M. 1987. Residential moves by elderly persons to U. S. central cities, suburbs, and rural areas. *Journal of Gerontology* 42: 534–539.

Golant, Stephen M. 1990. The metropolitanization and sub-urbanization of the U. S. elderly population: 1970–1988. *The Gerontologist* 30: 80–85.

Hendricks, Jon and Howard B. Turner. 1988. Social dimensions of mental illness among rural elderly populations. *International Journal of Aging and Human Development* 26: 169–190.

Kane, Robert L. and Rosalie A. Kane. 1990. Health care for older people: organizational and policy issues. In Robert H. Binstock and Linda K. George (eds.), *Handbook of Aging and the Social Sciences*. New York: Academic Press, 3rd edition.

Kim, Paul K. H. 1983. The rural elderly. In William P. Browne and Laura Katz Olson (eds.), *Aging and Public Policy*. Westport, CT: Greenwood.

Kivett, Vira R. 1985. Aging in rural society. In Raymond T. Coward and Gary

R. Lee (eds.), *The Elderly in Rural Society*. New York: Springer Publishing Company.

Krout, John A. 1986. *The Aged in Rural America*. Greenwich, CT: Greenwood Press.

Krout, John A. 1989. Rural versus urban differences in health dependence among the elderly population. *International Journal of Aging and Human Development* 28: 141–156.

Lassey, William R. and Marie L. Lassey. 1985. The physical health of the rural elderly. In Raymond T. Coward and Gary R. Lee (eds.), *The Elderly in Rural Society*. New York: Springer Publishing Company.

Lawton, M. Powell. 1985. The elderly in context: perspectives from environmental psychology and gerontology. *Environment and Behavior* 17: 501–519.

Lawton, M. Powell, M. Moss, and E. Moles. 1984. Pet ownership: a research note. *The Gerontologist* 24: 208–210.

Liang, J. 1982. Sex differences in life satisfaction among the elderly. *Journal of Gerontology* 37: 100–108.

Liang, J. and B. L. Warfel. 1983. Urbanism and life satisfaction among the aged. *Journal of Gerontology* 38: 97–106.

Longino, Charles F., Jr. 1990. Geographical distribution and migration. In Robert H. Binstock and Linda K. George (eds.), *Handbook of Aging and the Social Sciences*. New York: Academic Press.

McGhee, Jerrie L. 1983. Transportation opportunity and the rural elderly. *The Gerontologist* 23: 505–511.

Meddin, Jay and Alan Vaux. 1988. Subjective well-being among the rural elderly population. *International Journal of Aging and Human Development* 27: 193–206.

Menolascino, Frank J. and Jane F. Potter. 1989. Delivery of services in rural settings to the elderly mentally retarded-mentally ill. *International Journal of Aging and Human Development* 28: 261–275.

Nelson, Gary. 1980. Social services to the urban and rural aged. *The Gerontologist* 20: 200–207.

Norton, Lee and Mark C. Wozny. 1984. Residential location and nutritional adequacy among elderly adults. *Journal of Gerontology* 39: 592–595.

Okun, M. A. and W. A. Stock. 1987. Correlates and components of subjective well-being among the elderly. *Journal of Applied Gerontology* 6: 95–112.

Old Age and . . . 1980. *Old Age and Ruralism . . . A Case of Double Jeopardy*. Albany, N. Y.: New York Senate Research Service.

Palmore, Erdman. 1983. Health care needs of the rural elderly. *International Journal of Aging and Human Development* 18: 39–45.

Revicki, D. and Mitchell, J. P. 1990. Strain, social support, and mental health in rural elderly individuals. *Journal of Gerontology* 45: 267–274.

Scheidt, Rick J. 1985. The mental health of the aged in rural environments. In Raymond T. Coward and Gary R. Lee (eds.), *The Elderly in Rural Society*. New York: Springer Publishing Company.

Snow, R. and L. Crapo. 1982. Emotional bondedness, subjective well-being, and health in elderly medical patients. *Journal of Gerontology* 37: 609–615.

Speake, Diane L. and M. E. Cowart. 1988. The relationship between health behavior in rural and non-rural elderly. Presented at Gerontological Society of America, San Francisco.

Steiness, Donald and Timothy Hogan. 1992. Take the money and sun. *Journal of Gerontology* 47: s197–s203.

Stock, W. A. and M. A. Okun. 1982. The construct validity of life satisfaction among the elderly. *Journal of Gerontology* 37: 625–627.

Usui, W. M., T. J. Keil, and K. R. Durig. 1985. Socioeconomic comparisons and life satisfaction of elderly adults. *Journal of Gerontology* 40: 110–114.

Usui, W. M., T. J. Keil, and D. C. Phillips. 1983. Determinants of life satisfaction on a race-interaction hypothesis. *Journal of Gerontology* 38: 107–110.

Wagonfeld, M. O., H. F. Goldsmith, D. Stiles, and R. W. Manderscheid. 1988. In patient mental health services in metropolitan and non-metropolitan counties. *Journal of Rural Community Psychology* 9: 13–28.

Chapter 2

Methods of Data Gathering

Introduction

In this chapter, we discuss the basic data gathering techniques employed in two surveys of Allegany County, New York. The first was carried out in the summer of 1983 and the second in the summer of 1987. We compare the characteristics of Allegany County's rural elderly with the rural elderly generally, to see the extent to which our sample is "typical" or not.

Before we proceed further, a brief word about Allegany County itself is in order, so that the context within which these studies took place is clear. The county's population, according to the 1990 Census, is 50,470. The county is rural—there is not a single city within its boundaries. It is also a poor county. Median income, $24,164 per household, is among the lowest in New York State. 80% of the residents 18 years of age and older have a high school education; 16% have four years of college or more. However, the crime rate in the county is one of the lowest in New York State. The overall proportion of residents living under the poverty level in the County, according to the 1990 Census, is almost 15%. Most residents are white. Data indicate that 266 persons are black; 125 native American; 288 Asian; 96 "other." 370 persons are of Hispanic origin.

For older Americans, health care is important. Allegany County has two hospitals, both of which provide basic services to the elderly. The county's Office for the Aging aggressively seeks outreach to its constituency, although budgetary constraints make this a difficult undertaking.

Industry? Agriculture is a leading industry in this county. Of 15,100 persons employed in 1988, 3,300 were in manufacturing, 3,900 in

11

service industries, 3,900 in government work, 1,400 in education (there are four different colleges within the county, as well as other educational institutions), 2,600 in wholesale or retail, 300 in finance or real estate or insurance.

Leading employers include Dresser-Rand in Wellsville (the largest village in the county), manufacturer of steam turbines and generators; Air Preheater, producer of air preheaters, heat exchangers, and coal pulverizing equipment; Acme Electric in the village of Cuba, builders of voltage regulators, transformers, and battery chargers; Empire Cheese, Inc., producer of cheese. Of the 670,100 acres in the county, 204,600 are used for farming. There are 890 farms; the average size is 230 acres. However, much of the land is marginal.

All in all, Allegany County is a relatively poor, rural county. Services are available for the elderly. But because the county is poor and since there is a strong conservative ethos within the county, programs are not well funded and there is grudging approval for new program initiatives. It is within this context that the study took place.

1980 Census data provide greater detail about the elderly within Allegany County. The vast majority of elderly (60 and over) are white. Of the 8,211 persons 60 and over, only 62 were classified as black, native American, Asian-Pacific, or Hispanic. 25% live alone, says the 1980 Census, and 12% are below the poverty line. By 1990, the figures for the elderly had increased to 8,978 persons. Thus, given that the county's overall population declined, the proportion of elderly has actually increased over this period of time—from about 16% in 1980 to nearly 18% in 1990.

In the 1987 NORC General Social Survey, there are 107 respondents whom we classified as rural elderly. Their characteristics include the following:

1. More than half of the respondents have 10 years of education or less; the mode is a high school education;
2. Half those interviewed are 72 years of age or younger;
3. Sixty per cent of the sample are female;
4. Two per cent are black;
5. Modal income is between $10,000 to $14,999.

Below, we can use these findings to compare our sample's characteristics with the 1987 NORC results. This allows us to see the extent to which our respondents are representative of the rural elderly in general.

The 1983 Survey

In the summer of 1983, a set of trained interviewers went out into the field to interview a probability sample of Allegany County's older Americans. We used an amended form of the Older Americans' Status and Needs Assessment Questionnaire (Brukhardt and Lewis, 1975) (as we did also in 1987). 456 persons were interviewed. This represents an 82% response rate (number of respondents divided by number of respondents plus refusals). A proportionate stratified sample was used; over half of the towns in the county were included by this method. To ensure that people from all parts of the county and from the population centers would be included, we stratified by town size and by location (northern vs. southern half of the county).

Within towns thus selected, respondents were picked from a list of county residents aged 60 and over. The list contained about 3500 names and provided access to about 65% of the county's elderly population. The list was made up of persons contacting the local Office for the Aging or whose names came to the attention of that agency. There are several biases in this sample:

1. The sample includes the noninstitutionalized population. Although names of persons in hospitals and nursing homes were drawn, and attempts made to contact them, our interviewers were turned away repeatedly by administrators. The reason given was that normally the permission of a relative would have to be acquired by the administrators, and they claimed to be too busy to do this.
2. The sample is slightly older than the Census data report. The 1980 Census describes a mean age about 71.5 years; the sample's mean age is 74. This is probably due to the biases with the list provided us by the Office for the Aging, which has disproportionately few in the young-old category and a larger proportion in the old-old (75–84) category. Indeed, the local Office for the Aging has stated that the mailing list becomes more comprehensive and inclusive among older residents.
3. The sample is disproportionately female. 68% of the respondents are female and 32% are male. This is normal in survey research, since females are more accessible and more cooperative.

Next, we consider basic characteristics of the sample, and the conditions of life encountered by these people. As noted before, respondents average about 74 years of age. 44% of the people live alone. Almost everyone is white (99.3%; there is one native American in the sample). 44% are married. 55% of the sample had a high school diploma or beyond. The vast majority of people report having lived in their neighborhoods for 20 years or more—68%. 78% of the sample owned their own homes, with 12% of the respondents saying that their homes needed major repairs.

Transportation does not appear to be a major problem for most of the county's elderly. 89% report that they have little or no difficulties with transportation. Generally, people were satisfied with their lives. 48% say that they are very satisfied and 42% claim to be satisfied (thus, 90% of the respondents appear happy with their current circumstances).

The majority of the elderly interviewed here view themselves as well—only about 20% stated that their health was poor. 32% of the sample observe that they have had some substantial health problem the preceding year; thus, there seem to be more health problems than indicated by the self-reports of global health. The average respondent has about 1 ½ deficits in activities of daily living (ADLs). 49% have no such deficits. About 20% of the elderly contacted tell of some nutritional problem. The average income is about $7500 per year.

The 1987 Survey

A stratified random sample of county elderly was drawn from a list provided by the county's Office for the Aging. The list provided access to about ⅔ of the county's total elderly population. Of course, this by its very nature introduces some bias into our results. The list may underrepresent those who are worst off within the county, since they are the people least likely to be aware of and have made any kind of contact with the Office for the Aging (such contacts provide the basis for much of the mailing list). To reduce biases further (some parts of the county were overrepresented on the list and others—especially the northern, more rural half of the county—underrepresented), the sample was stratified by town, to ensure that enough respondents from the less populated areas would be included, and by region, to make sure that respondents from the northern part of the county appeared in the sample in numbers proportionate to their total presence in Allegany County.

In essence, then, the basic design was the same as it was in 1983.

The interviewing process began in late July and concluded in November, although the bulk of the interviewing was done by September. All in all, 358 usable interviews were completed.

Interviewers, hired and trained by the research team, reported no unusual problems in obtaining responses from those individuals willing to participate in the study. This is in contrast to the 1983 study, during which nursing homes refused access to our interviewing teams. In the 1987 study, however, the response rate (completed interviews divided by complete interviews plus refusals) was 72%, a percentage considered quite good by professional standards. Response rate is important, of course, because if it is excessively low, that may introduce biases into the study.

Next, we give a brief summary of the characteristics of Allegany County's elderly as of 1987 and some of the situations that they face in their everyday lives. 64% of the respondents are female and 36% male. As in 1983, females are disproportionately represented (regrettably, this is not uncommon in survey research, since females are more apt to respond to questionnaires). The average age of respondents is 75, slightly higher than the census figures for 1980. This is probably due to the fact that the sample was drawn from the Office for the Aging's mailing list, which includes those who have sought assistance. The old-old, 75 to 84, are more likely to use programs; hence, something of an upward bias with respect to age. Nonetheless, the age of our respondents is not so much greater than the Census figures as to raise serious questions about the sample's representativeness.

The education level, on average, is having finished high school. Additionally, people who were interviewed have deep roots in their geographical areas; the average person has lived in his or her home about twenty years. The median income is only about $7000. The sample, then, is not wealthy; however, most people feel that they have enough resources to meet their basic needs.

Conditions of life include such things as health status, ability to carry out activities of daily living, housing situation, and so on. In the next several paragraphs, we will summarize the ordinary lives of Allegany County's elderly as of 1987.

First, health status. Overall, the respondents are healthy. A slight majority (52%) say that they lost no days of normal activity during the preceding year from illness. 13%, though, did lose one or more months of normal activity. This is a minority, but it is sizable. Respondents were also asked about deficits in activities of daily living, such as clipping toenails, bathing, reading, and so on. About two thirds report no deficits, whereas 12% complain of two or more. At the conclusion of the interview, our trained interviewers noted on the questionnaire whether or not the person just spoken with had any significant infirmities, such as blindness, extreme obesity, mobility problems, tremors, and the like. 72% of those interviewed were judged to be free of any significant infirmities; 28% had at least one. 14% of the people were assessed as having two or more. Thus, while health is pretty good for the rural elderly reported upon in this volume, there are many who do suffer from a variety of ailments. It is worth noting, in addition, that 9% of the people interviewed claim that they had unmet health care problems, a substantial proportion of the sample.

Given the number of older citizens with one or more ADL deficits, it is unsurprising that 8% indicate a desire to move to ". . . an affordable, maintenance free, supervised facility." Another question ascertained the need for in home care expressed by respondents. About one person out of five indicates that, if he or she were sick or disabled, there would be no one to care for them. More directly, 20% of the respondents stated that they or their spouses need some kind of in-home care. About 4% of the sample claim to need some sort of adult day care, for respite from a family member with some debilitating disease (such as Alzheimer's Disease).

A final aspect of medical care is personality dysfunction. Two survey scales (shortened versions of Costa and McCrae's scales) were designed to determine the extent to which respondents were "neurotic" or "depressed." About 8% responded with three or more answers per scale that registered depression; 11% indicated a similar level of neuroticism. Only 5% of the elderly have ever received counseling, by the way, which suggests a gap between need and use of services.

Other aspects of their lives. . . . 26% of the respondents claim to have one or more problems with transportation (such as not having a car in working order or not being able to get around when the person wants to). 32% say that they have one or more social needs (such as being lonely, not seeing other people as often as they wished), 69% assert that they face one or more housing problems (such as water often getting into the basement, keeping the thermostat set very low, needing major repairs). Poor nutrition seems to face about 15% of the sample. 21% of the people interviewed note that they have problems paying for major items such as prescription drugs, food, heating, and medical bills. 35% are below the poverty line and 44% are near poor.

Still and all, given the recitation of difficulties, the residents find their life quite satisfying. One question asked was the global index of life satisfaction, "Taking everything into consideration, how would you describe your satisfaction with life at the present time. . . . ?" 47% reply that they are very satisfied and 42% that they are satisfied. Thus, 89% of the respondents appear to be happy with how their lives are going (of course, there are considerable problems with this single metric of satisfaction; but we return to that in a later chapter).

Discussion

Overall, the characteristics of our samples are not decidedly distinct from those of national samples. Compared with NORC results, those interviewed in 1983 and 1987 are somewhat older, more apt to be female, slightly more educated, and a little poorer. Additionally, results are not too dissimilar from those reported by Shanas (1982). Thus, we can have some confidence that the samples used here are not particularly atypical of rural elderly in general.

References

Brukhardt, J. E. and J. C. Lewis. 1975. *The Older Americans' Status and Needs Assessment Questionnaire*. Washington, D. C.: Department of Health, Education, and Welfare.

Shanas, E. 1982. *National Survey of the Aged*. Washington, D. C.: Department of Health and Human Services.

Chapter 3
Public Lives, Part I:
Political Orientations and Behavior

Introduction

Studying the political behavior of the elderly is an increasingly important question. If we accept the definition of the elderly as those who are 65 and older, this age group now constitutes some 12% (about 27 million) of the U.S. population. By the year 2000, they will number almost 32 million; by 2030 some 21% of Americans will fall into this category (Longino, Soldo, and Manton, 1990). But impressive as they are, these figures actually *understate* the potential strength of the elderly as an electoral force—for two reasons. One, there will be many others who will probably have much the same political objectives. We refer here to the "near-aged"—that very sizable group composed of early retirees, of those nearing retirement, and of their spouses (Binstock, 1972). Even though the great majority of these individuals will not have reached the magic 65 milestone, they will share most of the concerns of those who have, pushing the 20% potential electoral strength figure considerably higher. Two, the elderly turn out to vote at a higher level than most other age cohorts. For instance, in 1988, 68.8% of those 65 and over who were eligible to vote reported exercising their franchise; for the population as a whole, the corresponding figure is 57.4%. In fact, those from 65 to 74 years old had the highest turnout rates of all age cohorts reported upon—73% ("Democracy is ageless," 1991).

Given a steadily maturing population, the elderly are also likely to constitute a growing proportion of our political elite, i.e., of legislators, elected members of the executive branches of government and the

19

judiciary, at all levels of government. It is quite possible that, as the age of mandatory retirement is raised or even eliminated, they will constitute an even larger proportion of our bureaucracies.

There is yet a third factor which makes the political behavior of the aged a matter of increasing importance. We can now see emerging a number of political issues in which our older citizens will have very substantial interest. Among these are social security, medical care, housing, age discrimination, and "right to die" legislation. Even now there is mounting concern over the future of the retirement provisions of the Social Security program, as the ratio of retirees to workers (whose payments presumably will support the system) rapidly rises (for a "worst case" scenario, see Easterlin, 1978).

In short, there are three very practical reasons why the political behavior of the aged has been and continues to be a matter of scholarly attention: the elderly constitute an already sizable and rapidly growing percentage of our population and, more to the point, of our electorate; they will, in all likelihood, comprise a larger proportion of our political elite, in all branches and at all levels of government; many of the major issues facing our society in the coming years will be those in which the elderly will have a very direct personal interest. Clearly, then, the manner in which aging influences political behavior is a matter of considerable importance to our society.

In this chapter, we examine one aspect of rural older Americans' public lives—their political orientations and behavior, and the network of factors that affect these. We begin by summarizing the extant literature on political behavior of older Americans, with special emphasis on those living in rural areas (although little research is broken down this way). We will use our two Allegany County surveys to get a portrait of just what the political views of rural elderly are. Then, we explain the considerable variation in political orientations and behavior. We consider both standard, mainstream predictor variables as well as some less traditional, but still important ones, such as health status, personality, and life satisfaction.

Simply, little has been done on this specific aspect of political gerontology. We can say a great deal about the behavior of the elderly in general, but not so much about the rural elderly. To provide some context for the following discussion, we summarize (a) the mainstream view of explaining political orientations and behavior, (b) some basic findings about the elderly, (c) findings about those living in rural areas.

The Mainstream Explanation

Before exploring the linkages among predictors and political orientations and activity among older Americans, though, a little background is needed. Cutler (1977) contends that two key variables shaping political views of the elderly are education and group consciousness (see also Cutler and Schmidhauser, 1975). As with other age groups, increased education goes along with more participatory orientations, such as political interest, level of political knowledge, sense of political efficacy (that is, extent to which one thinks oneself to be an effective political actor) and behavior (Milbrath and Goel, 1977). This unsurprising fact assumes significance because the educational level of the elderly is increasing progressively and will continue to do so as better educated cohorts move into the ranks of the aged (see Williamson et al, 1982). Verba and Nie (1972) report that group consciousness helps to boost levels of participatory predispositions and behavior. Just so, Cutler (1977) contends that increased group consciousness among the elderly can produce more political activity. Thus, two key predictors of political participation among the elderly are education and a sense of group consciousness, both of which appear to be rising, suggesting even greater activism in the future.

Let us now examine the relationship of age with a number of political orientations (general beliefs about the political system) and behaviors (from voting to contributing to a campaign) (for a fuller survey, see Somit and Peterson, 1990; Hudson and Strate, 1985; Jacobs, 1990).

Politics and the Elderly

Political Participation

The standard interpretation used to be that participation peaks in later middle age and then declines fairly rapidly with age (e.g., Milbrath and Goel, 1977). Later studies suggested that when education is taken into account, participation actually increases until people reach well into their 70s (Wolfinger and Rosenstone, 1980. Cf. Verba and Nie, 1972; Nie, Verba, and Kim, 1974). A recent study shows that participation in terms of voting in elections begins to decline at 67 (for the non-college educated) and at 57 (for the college educated) (Strate et al., 1989; and see Jennings and Markus, 1988). For more active kinds of participation, the decline is greater (Jennings and Markus, 1988). All in all, though, participation is higher among the elderly than many might think.

Political Orientations

Alienation. A series of studies indicate that with greater age goes increased political alienation (distrust in government, sense of powerlessness) (Gilmour and Lamb, 1975; Abramson, 1983; Agnello, 1973; Williamson et al., 1982).

Political tolerance. With increased age goes a small diminution in extent of tolerance toward politically unpopular groups (Sullivan, Piereson, and Marcus, 1982).

Political efficacy. Older Americans are more apt to have a lower sense of political efficacy (Abramson, 1983), with the decline being rather substantial (Jennings and Markus, 1988).

Political ideology. The simple description is that older people are more conservative (Lipset, 1960; Campbell, 1979; Erikson et al., 1991). However, more detailed analysis of the relationship shows that the correlation between age and ideology is not so clearcut (e.g., Hudson and Strate, 1985). For instance, on "life style" issues, the elderly are more conservative (Miller and Levitin, 1976; Lupfer and Rosenberg, 1983), whereas they are more liberal on aging issues (e.g., Medicare) (Cutler and Schmidhauser, 1975). Overall, aging **by itself** does not seem to lead to conservative beliefs (see especially Glenn and Hefner, 1972). On the other hand, older people tend to be somewhat more ideologically sophisticated (Jennings and Markus, 1988).

Partisanship. Two aspects of party identification merit consideration: strength of identification and actual party preference. Study after study concludes that strength of identification increases with age (Miller and Levitin, 1976; Campbell et al., 1964; Hudson and Strate, 1985). To the extent that there is change in party identification, it tends to be much less in the parental than younger (Baby Boom) generation, according to Jennings' three-wave survey of 1965 high school students and their parents (Jennings and Markus, 1984). One specific index of this is reduced ticket-splitting (DeVries and Tarrance, 1972). Direction of identification? Glenn and Hefner (1972) find no particular impact of aging itself on party choice.

Political involvement. Surveys of extant literature conclude that interest in politics increases with age (Hudson and Strate, 1985), although political knowledge does not appear to go up (Jennings and

Markus, 1988). Strate et al. (1989) report that political involvement (interest plus knowledge) steadily increases with age until about 67 (for non-college educated) and the late 50s (for college educated).

Rural Elderly: Baseline Data on Their Political Behavior

National data

The preceding discussion outlines what research tells us about the political lives of older Americans. However, none of the studies further breaks out the rural elderly. To get a sense of the effects of rural residence on Older Americans' political orientations and behavior, we use the 1987 National Opinion Research Center (NORC) General Social Survey (GSS).

We consider the effects of ruralness on three different categories of people's political orientations and behavior: politicization (extent of political involvement), alienation (dissatisfaction with the current order and sense of isolation from the larger world), and ideology. A brief word about the different measures is in order.

The sample that we use is the 1987 National Opinion Research Center (NORC) General Social Survey (GSS). The overall sample size (not counting the black oversample carried out that year) is 1466 persons. Of these, 359 are 60 years of age and older, that segment of the data base that we examine in the pages to come. The General Social Survey is a probability sample of Americans; hence, we are not as subject to problems of external validity as if we had used a more idiosyncratic, less representative sample. The measures used are:

Ideology. Several indicators of ideology are employed. One was ideological self-identification. People were asked to rank themselves on a scale of 1 (extremely liberal) to 7 (extremely conservative). A second indicator is political party identification. Respondents rated themselves on a gradient ranging from strongly Democratic to strongly Republican (the measure is the Survey Research Center's familiar item). A third metric of liberal views is agreement with the statement that ". . . government is obligated to help blacks." Fourth, a measure of tolerance toward unpopular groups (e.g., atheists, socialists, racists, communists, militarists, gays) was constructed via a summed index. A final barometer of ideology is a summed index, called "Life style liberalism." Here, we assessed the extent to which individuals could be said to hold "liberal" positions on life style issues, i.e., acceptance of homosexual relations, acceptance of premarital sexual relations, opposition to strict pornography laws (these items were selected on grounds of both common sense and the results of reliability analysis—support for abortion dropped out when results for this issue were examined).

Alienation. A number of items are likewise used to represent alienation. One is a short form of Srole's anomie index (Cronbach's alpha = .51; standardized item alpha = .51). Another indicator, regarded as one of the most important measures of alienation (Inglehart, 1990), is a short version of Rosenberg's misanthropy scale (a Cronbach's alpha of .33; standardized item alpha = .34). A more directly political scale is a summed index of confidence in political institutions, constituted by three questions that asked if respondents had a great deal of confidence in the executive branch of the federal government, the United States Supreme Court, and the Congress. Those responses indicating confidence were added up to produce a summed index (Cronbach's alpha = .54; standardized item alpha = .54). Alienation is further measured by responses to the following three questions:

(1) Agreement (or disagreement) that ". . . you can trust the local government . . . almost never";

(2) Agreement (or disagreement) that ". . . people like you can have [no] influence over local government decisions";

(3) Agreement (or disagreement) that ". . . you can trust the government in Washington . . . almost never."

Politicization. Several measures serve to register level of politicization. One of these is the extent to which people are ". . . interested in politics and national affairs . . ." Another is the extent to which people ". . . read the newspaper every day . . ." Information level is an important aspect of politicization. The NORC questionnaire asks whether or not people know the name of the governor of their state, their member of the U. S. House of Representatives, and the head of their local school system. An index was formed to reflect degree of political information: if a respondent knew all three, his/her score would be 3; if a person knew none of the incumbents, the score would be 0 (Cronbach's alpha = .61; standardized item alpha = .61).

Finally, there is an index of political participation. This is based on the Verba and Nie (1972) questions. People were asked whether or not—or to what extent—they participated in the following: "worked with others in the community to try to solve some community problems," "taken part in forming a new group or a new organization to try to solve some community problems," "try to show people why they should vote for one of the parties or candidates,'' ''work for one of the parties or candidates,'' ''attended any political meetings or rallies,'' ''gone to see, or spoken to, or written to some member of local government,'' ''contacted or written . . . some representatives or government officials outside of the local community,'' vote regularly in local elections, voted in the 1984 presidential election, ''contributed money to a political party or candidate or to any other political cause.'' If the person reported contacting an official either within local government or outside the local community, that individual was then asked if the contact were about a community problem or about a personal problem particular to the individual. A summed index was created, indicating the number of different activities engaged in. Cronbach's alpha for this index is a healthy .73 (standardized item alpha = .74).

The political participation scale, though, has normally been found to be composed of a series of distinct dimensions that unfold through factor analysis (e.g., see Verba and Nie, 1972). Factor analysis of the preceding specific questions about participation yields a factor solution very similar to the one reported in Verba and Nie (1972). Four additional summed indices were created corresponding to each of the dimensions isolated in the factor analysis: (1) campaign politics (the extent to which individuals report trying to influence others' votes, working for a party or candidate, and contributing money to a party or candidate); (2) communal politics (contact with public officials about some community problem); (3) particularized contacting (extent of contacts with public officials to advance some special interest); (4) voting (voting in local elections and reported having voted in the 1984 election).

Table 3.1 summarizes the network of relationships between place of residence (rural *versus* nonrural) and the political variables.

Pearson's correlation coefficients show that: rural residence is associated with greater levels of particularistic contacting, somewhat more anomie, greater confidence in American political institutions, more trust in the federal government, Republican partisan identification, less tolerance for unpopular groups, and less support for the national government helping blacks. In short, rural residents may be, overall, a bit less alienated (with the exception of somewhat greater anomie) and more conservative. However, zero-order correlations can be misleading. Next, we discuss the findings when controls for age, sex, education, income, and group memberships are introduced.

Betas (standardized regression coefficients) in Table 3.1 show that the relationships described in the previous paragraph generally hold

Table 3.1. Multiple Regression: Rural Residence as a Predictor of Sociopolitical Variables of Those 60 and Over, 1987 NORC Data, N = 292.

	Rural	
	r	Beta
Politicization		
Political participation	.05	.09*
Campaign politics	− .05	− .03
Communal politics	.01	.05
Contacting	.11**	.12**
Voter participation	.02	.06
Follows news regularly	− .02	.06
Political interest	.05	.09
Political information	.04	.08
Alienation		
Anomie	.08*	.04
Misanthropy	.06	.03
Confidence in political institutions	.10**	.11*
Trust in federal government	.15***	.16***
Trust in local government	.06	.07
Influence over local government	.07	.09*
Ideology		
Republican identification	.09*	.12**
Conservative ideology	.03	.03
Tolerant	− .18****	− .12**
Government help for blacks	− .15***	− .14**
Life style liberalism	− .04	− .03
Control Variables		
Education	− .18***	
Age	.10*	
Female	− .03	
Number of group memberships	.01	

*   P < .10
**   P < .05
***   P < .01
****P < .001

up. Indeed, some of the zero-order relationships actually get stronger, further strengthening the case that rural residence is an independent factor in understanding political orientations and behavior. The overall index of political participation comes to be somewhat higher for those living in rural areas, and contacting remains affected by rurality. Those residing in rural locales are also more apt to trust the federal government, have confidence in national political institutions, have a sense of influence over their local governments, be more Republican, less tolerant, and less supportive of the national government helping blacks. Thus, it does appear that where one lives has an effect on political orientations and behavior. More detailed analysis of the factors shaping the rural elderly's political behavior is thereby warranted. To do this, we use data from our surveys of Allegany County.

Allegany County data

Table 3.2 reports on the baseline "socioeconomic model" results for Allegany County (using the 1987 data base). Here, we report the extent to which several standard independent variables—sex, age, education, income, and group memberships—are associated with a series of dependent variables.

Dependent variables include internal political efficacy (the sense that

Table 3.2. Standardized Regression Coefficients, Multiple Regression: Predicting Political Variables, 1987 Allegany County Data Base, N = 261.

	Traditional Predictors						
	Group member-ships	*Age*	*Female*	*Income*	*Years of education*	*R*	*R square*
Political interest	.23**	.03	− .09	.11*	.14**	.40	.16
Internal efficacy	.08	.08	.05	.19**	.21**	.39	.15
Political participation	.19**	.12**	− .03	.32**	.23**	.60	.36
Republican	.19**	.12*	.10*	− .16	.06	.26	.07
Conservative	.09	.02	.09	− .11	− .12	.20	.04
Trust in national government	.15**	.00	.03	− .10	.07	.18	.03

* P < .10
**P < .05

one can have an effect on government), political interest (extent to which one follows government and public affairs), political participation (a summed index, indicating the number of activities engaged in by individuals, such as "worked with others in the community to try to solve some community problem," "worked for a candidate for office," contacted a bureaucrat or bureaucracy about some problem," "contributed money to a political cause"), conservative ideological identification (individuals rated themselves on a 7-point scale from 1 = extremely conservative to 7 = extremely liberal), Republican partisan identification, trust in government ("How much of the time do you think that you can trust the government in Washington to do the right thing?" and "Would you say that the government is pretty much run by a few big interests looking out for themselves or that it is run for the benefit of all the people?").

Betas from listwise multiple regression analysis depict the following: more *group memberships* go with increasing political interest, more political participation, identifying oneself as Republican, and trusting the federal government; *age* is associated with more participation and greater likelihood of defining oneself as Republican; *females* are more likely to see themselves as Republican; *higher income* correlates with more political interest, efficacy, and political action; *more years of education* predict greater interest, efficacy, and participation. In subsequent analysis, the results of Table 2 stand as a kind of baseline against which to compare the effects of other variables on political behavior.

Health as an Explanatory Variable

Health Status. It seems reasonable to speculate that health influences political behavior. Someone who is seriously ill, for example, is ordinarily less able to engage in such activity. It seems reasonable to suggest that, in fact, health status can influence political behavior. Someone who is seriously ill, for example, is frequently less able to engage in "outside" activities. In addition, those who are ill may adopt a "sickness role" (Sanders, 1982; Parsons, 1951; Mechanic, 1965), in which they are considered exempt from normal obligations, including, we might speculate, political involvement. Such a role is frequently associated with passivity, a greater sense of helplessness, and reduced social functioning. Being sick also reduces one's sense of competence and well-being (Mechanic and Hansell, 1987). All of this would predict reduced political activity.

David Schwartz (1976a, 1976b, 1978; Schwartz et al., 1975) has conducted several studies of the relationship between health and political activity, using a national adult sample, high school students in New Jersey, adults in the urban northeast, members of Congress, top-level administrators in Washington, D.C., and federal appeals court judges. He finds that poorer health is associated with depressed levels of participation, more negative views toward the political world, and more passive views toward politics. Alan Booth and Susan Welch (1976) rely on fairly complete health data (derived from a medical examination) for a Toronto sample and detect some modest relationship with political activity—but in a direction contrary to Schwartz' findings. Alan McBride (1980) replicated Schwartz' research on a sample of Southern Illinois students, but he was unable to confirm Schwartz' results (see also Peterson, 1974).

National Opinion Research Center data from 1982 and 1984 show that healthier people are somewhat less alienated from politics, somewhat more conservative, and more interested in politics, even though the associations are modest indeed (Peterson, 1988, 1990). Data from 1987 suggest that better health translates into more politically active citizens (Peterson, 1991a).

Prior research says that health status has some effect on individuals' political lives, although there are mixed signals provided by the literature. Since one consequence of the aging process is diminished physical and—in some cases—mental powers, effects of health problems might be more dramatic among the elderly.

The data set used to investigate the purported relationship is the 1987 survey of 358 rural older Americans in upstate New York (for a report on biosocial predictors of political orientations and behavior using the 1983 data set, see Peterson, 1987b).

Scholars have long contended that biological factors have impacts on the behavior of the elderly (e.g., G. Schubert, 1983a; but cf. Rowe and Kahn, 1988). Campbell, Converse, Miller, and Stokes note that decline of voter turnout with age is (1960:262) ''. . . undoubtedly due to infirmities that make trips to the polling place more difficult.'' Hudson and Binstock suggest that lowered political participation (1976:370) ''. . . may be interpreted in terms of physical decline. . . .'' Light thinks that (1981:2343) ''Health and mobility problems apparently prevent the elderly from topping the middle-aged in turnout.'' On the other hand, Wolfinger and Rosenstone (1980) find that with the introduction of controls for length of residence, income, education, and gender, effects of aging on political activity seem to disappear. However, outside of one study based on our 1983 data (Peterson, 1987b) and a second using NORC data from 1987 (Peterson and Somit, 1990), there has been no real test of the postulated relationship between health status and political behavior of the elderly—and the first exception involved a very limited number of political dependent variables.

Hypotheses. Based upon literature already discussed, we expect that, as health problems increase, levels of political interest, political efficacy, and political participation will all decline. These are straightforward predictions based on previous work.

Also, poorer health might lead to less of a status quo view, and, as a result, less conservatism and less identification with the Republican party. Why would this be so? Schwartz (1976) contends that less healthy people will be more oriented toward social and political change and more desirous of reform. Their poorer health, in a sense, moves them to wish for change in their body's functioning and this spills over to a desire for political change. Conservatives and Republicans tend to be less oriented toward reform. Hence, we expect less healthy people to be less conservative and Republican, to adhere less to the status quo.

Thus, as health level decreases, the probability of being conservative decreases and of being Republican goes down.

Poor health can raise questions in a person's mind about how fair and meaningful the world is. This could translate into anomie and alienation. Further predictions, then, include the following: as health status diminishes, alienation increases (one index of alienation is cynicism about government). Some preliminary work using a variety of samples (see Peterson, 1987a; 1990) suggests that poorer health ought to be tied to less trust in government (one dimension of alienation). Schwartz' work also seems to point to these hypotheses as reasonable expectations.

Methods. A test of these hypotheses comes from data on the 1987 sample of 358 older Americans. The indicators of health status are:

Physical infirmities:
[Instructions to interviewers] "Did the interviewee have any of the following conditions?
Blindness
Deafness
Missing limbs

Obesity
Palsy, tremor, shakes
Speech impediments
Mobility problems."

After having added up the total number of problems for each person, we then dichotomized the variable (0 = no problems; 1 = one or more problems).

Sick days:
Self-report of number of days of restricted activity over the past year due to health problems.

Health problems index:
A summed index indicating extent of health problems. Components include:
Sick days,
"Have not been well most of the time,"
Having one or more physical infirmities.

Needless to say, there are problems with self-reports of health (See, e.g., Kobassa, 1982; Wolinsky, 1980; Brunswick, 1977). However, there is abundant evidence that self-reports can be both reliable and valid metrics of health status, and that self-assessments are positively associated with physicians' diagnoses, medical record data, differential mortality, presence of chronic conditions, change in objective health status, and the use of doctors (e.g., see Garrity, 1978; Fillenbaum, 1979; Ware, 1986; Ferraro, 1980; Kaplan, Barell, and Lusky, 1988; Idler and Kasl, 1991; Rodin and McAvay, 1992; Wolinsky and Johnson, 1992; Sherbourne and Meredith, 1992). Although self-ratings—including global "feeling state" (the term comes from Baumann, 1961)—are sometimes criticized as too subjective, unreliable, and invalid, the results seem to speak otherwise (Ware, 1986).

The two control variables are years of education and group consciousness, here operationalized as a "yes" answer to the question "Are you a member of any local or national organizations for older Americans?" These two were selected for the reasons outlined by Cutler, already noted above (1977).

Findings. Table 3.3 presents the matrix of Pearson's correlation coefficients for the sample of rural elderly. Dependent variables are political efficacy, political interest, a participation index, liberalism,

Table 3.3 Partial Correlation Analysis: Political Orientations and Behavior by Health Measures, N = 302 (controlling education and "group consciousness").

	Sickdays		*Physical Infirmities*		*Health Problems Index*	
	r	*Partial*	*r*	*Partial*	*r*	*Partial*
Political efficacy	−.08*	−.07	−.20****	−.17***	−.19****	−.16**
Political interest	−.21****	−.21****	−.29****	−.26****	−.23****	−.20****
Political participation	−.05	−.03	−.16***	−.11**	−.12**	−.07*
Conservatism	.02	.03	−.09*	−.08*	−.05	−.03
Approval of Ronald Reagan	−.11**	−.11**	−.08*	−.07*	−.14***	−.13**
Republican identification	−.09*	−.08*	−.14***	−.13**	−.10**	−.09*
Trust in government	−.11**	−.10**	.00	.01	−.09*	−.07
Internal locus of control	−.20****	−.20****	−.33****	−.27****	−.34****	−.32****

```
 *    P < .10
 **   P < .05
 ***  P < .01
****P < .001
```

approval of Ronald Reagan, Republican party identification, trust in government, and internal locus of control.

The health indices have some association with dependent variables as the table shows. Number of sick days goes with lower efficacy, less political interest, diminished approval of Ronald Reagan, less Republican identification, and less trust in government. Number of physical infirmities is an even stronger correlate; it goes with lower levels of all the following—efficacy, interest, participation, conservatism, approval of President Reagan, and Republican partisanship. The health problems index also seems to depress efficacy, interest, participation, Reagan approval, Republican identification, and trust in government.

Zero-order correlations, though, may be misleading. Table 3.3 also presents partial correlation coefficients. Control variables are education and "group consciousness," operationalized as membership in an organization for older Americans, such as AARP. The health measures are related to some but not all variables as predicted. No indicator of health is tied to conservatism, with controls in place. Only one is associated with political participation or trust in government. Two of the four metrics predict to less political efficacy. Three are associated with lower levels of approval for Ronald Reagan. All four variables are linked with lower interest, less Republican identification, and an external locus of control. The statistically significant findings are in predicted directions. The most effective health predictor is the index of physical infirmities. While the impact of health variables is reduced with the introduction of controls, effects do remain, especially for the presence of any physical infirmities. The findings suggest that health has a role to play in older Americans' political orientations and behavior.

To get a better sense of the nexus of relations, a regression-based path analysis was conducted, with political participation as dependent variable. This was selected because of its clear importance as an influence in politics (e.g., Verba and Nie, 1972). A summed index, civic orientations, was created for this analysis. A person got one point if judged efficacious and a second if indicating a strong interest in politics. Our assumptions were that civic orientations, education level, physical infirmities, and group consciousness would all have a direct impact on participation; infirmities, group consciousness, and education would shape civic orientations; infirmities and education would influence group consciousness; education would be tied to less physical infirmity. Figure 3.1 illustrates the results of path analysis based upon these assumptions. Only paths significant at .05 or less are included. The path coefficients represent the betas (standardized regression coefficients) from stepwise multiple regression.

As one can see, the model shows that the health measure has an indirect—but not a direct effect—on participation. Nonetheless, extent of individuals' physical problems does influence—through its impact on civic orientations—the level of participation in politics. In this manner, greater health problems are associated with a diminution in political participation and, as one result, a less powerful political voice.

Summary and discussion. Basic findings are easily summarized:

1. Poorer health among older Americans is associated with greater liberalism, more alienation, lower levels of political interest, efficacy, and participation. These relationships are weakened, but still maintain a statistically significant relationship with the introduction of controls.
2. A path analysis shows clearly that one metric of poor health has

Figure 3.1. Path Model: Predicting Political Participation (N = 345).

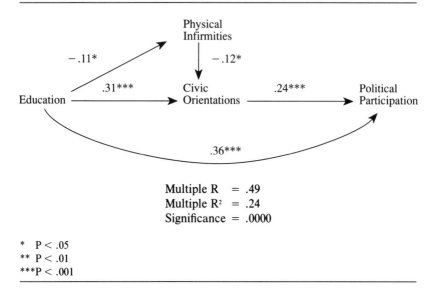

Multiple R = .49
Multiple R² = .24
Significance = .0000

*   P < .05
** P < .01
***P < .001

an indirect effect on political participation consistent with expectations.

Results, then, are supportive of the hypotheses advanced earlier. So what? Political participation is a potentially powerful weapon in the hands of an aroused populace. Any number of studies show that political participation can make a difference in decision-making (Verba and Nie, 1972). However, it has also been shown that this introduces, *par consequence*, subtle biases into representative mechanisms. Those who are most active have the greatest voice; those who are most active also happen to be the better educated and those from higher socioeconomic strata (Verba and Nie, 1972). The result, simply, is "them what has, gets."

Among older Americans, results suggest that something similar may be going on. The least healthy among the aging are least likely to follow politics and to get involved in politics. Their political views are distinct from the healthier; the least healthy are more apt to be liberal and Democratic. However, they are also less active and less interested in politics and more alienated from the political system. By not being involved more, their voices will not be heard. In the end, this will reduce the odds that their views will be listened to. This introduces a possible bias into a representative system. So what, then? Health status, as predictor of political orientations and behavior, becomes one more variable to consider in understanding the nature of politics in a democratic society that can work to exclude the least fortunate sectors of society.

Furthermore, as we noted in Chapter 1, the rural elderly rate their health less positively than their non-rural peers. To the extent that perceptions of health status, then, affect political participation, the rural elderly may have a less effective political voice than other elderly. Rural older Americans have lower income and education to begin with; combine that with poorer self-reported health and the result is a muted political voice. To the extent that our findings could be generalized to other rural elderly, this becomes an important issue to explore.

Personality and Political Behavior

Interest in examining the role of personality generally in adult development has waxed and waned over the years. Recently, however, there has been renewed interest in personality change and adult development (McCrae and Costa, 1984). Past research on personality and aging, more specifically, has looked at the influence of personality on a wide range of issues—from its role in decision making to its impact on social activity and well-being among the elderly. Very little research, though, has focused on the influence of personality variables on the political activity of the aged population, despite the fact that the elderly are quite politically active (Wolfinger and Rosenstone, 1980) and are currently the fastest growing segment of our population—suggesting the importance of carefully exploring those factors, including personality, that shape the political orientations and behavior of this age cohort.

The study of personality and politics itself has generated much research (see, for instance, Greenstein, 1975; Stone, 1974; Knutson, 1973), although there are also serious problems clarifying the nature of the linkage (Greenstein, 1969). In this part of the chapter, we explore the impact of basic personality variables on the political orientations and behavior of a sample of rural older Americans. First, though, we limited the scope of our measures of personality; we restrict our study of personality and politics to three *trait* factors (extroversion, openness, and neuroticism) and one measure of *self-concept* (locus of control).

Traits are defined as the enduring set of characteristics or dispositions that determine interpersonal, experiential, attitudinal, and emotional styles (McCrae and Costa, 1988). Past research has shown that a taxonomy of five trait factors are important for understanding personality (Norman, 1963). These factors include extroversion, agreeableness, conscientiousness, emotional stability, and culture. From these five factors, we selected three traits having been well-established and the original domains assessed by the NEO Inventory.

Personality variables. First, we examine the nature of each of these personality variables. Then, we go ahead and summarize the literature that relates these to political orientations and behavior.

The three trait variables are defined and assessed via the NEO Inventory (e.g., see Costa and McCrae, 1985; McCrae and Costa, 1988). Individuals high on the NEO scale of neuroticism display considerable levels of anxiety, depression, and other forms of negative affect. On the contrary, extroverted individuals are optimistic, see themselves in a positive light, and are highly sociable. They are also assertive, active, talkative people who like excitement and are attracted to groups.

Open individuals reflect the elements of active imagination, aesthetic sensitivity, receptiveness to inner feelings, preference for variety, intellectual curiosity, and independence of judgment. Openness is modestly related to high levels of intelligence and education.

Our fourth personality indicator, locus of control, deals with self-concept. It registers the extent to which a person feels that he or she has control over their life and environment (internal) or the degree to which they are controlled by their environments (external). Those with an internal locus of control bring with them a sense of mastery over themselves and their environment. They emanate confidence and competence; they are in control.

A number of studies have assessed the political impacts of these personality dimensions upon people's political orientations and behavior. These studies essentially focus on the general population, but they provide the basis for hypotheses about the effects of personality on older Americans' political behavior.

Locus of control. A number of studies suggest that an external locus of control goes with less knowledge about and interest in politics (Knutson, 1973). Internal locus of control, not surprisingly, predicts lower levels of political discontent and increased political efficacy (Milbrath and Goel, 1977), although its relationship to actual political participation is not very straightforward (Stone, 1981).

Extroversion. The more extroverted a person, the more apt that individual is to have elevated political efficacy (Milbrath and Goel, 1977), to be "tough minded" (Stone, 1974), and to be less alienated from the political system (Hughes, 1975). In addition, some studies suggest that extroverted people tend to be more active in their political behavior (Milbrath and Goel, 1977).

Openness. Openness, as here defined, has similarity to the "open minded" end of Milton Rokeach's open-minded close-minded continuum. Existing research suggests that dogmatism (or closed minded personality) is associated with conservatism (Elizabeth and Peterson, 1984; Stone, 1980), racism (Elizabeth and Peterson, 1984; Stone, 1980), intolerance (Sullivan et al., 1982; Rokeach, 1960), diminished interpersonal trust (Stone, 1980), lower political efficacy (Stone, 1974), lower information levels (implied in Fiske et al., 1983), and reduced political participation (Stone, 1974).

Neuroticism. What little evidence there is suggests that neuroticism goes with greater political alienation and more ethnocentric attitudes (Hughes, 1975). Negative affect (for instance, being depressed) is associated with less protest participation (Milbrath and Goel, 1977), greater political apathy and reduced levels of traditional participation (implied in Mussen and Wyszinski, 1952).

Hypotheses. A series of hypotheses applying specifically to older Americans emerges from our discussion above:

As internal locus of control increases, we hypothesize that political efficacy will increase, that political interest will increase, that political distrust will decrease, that status quo orientation will increase, and that political participation will increase. Most of these follow clearly from extant literature.

As extroversion increases, political efficacy will increase, political interest will increase, political distrust will decrease, status quo orientation will increase, and political participation will increase. Most of these are simple extrapolations from the literature earlier cited. The predicted impact on political interest makes sense, since as one is more outwardly oriented, one is more likely to be aware of the environment and show some interest in it. That is, one is able to "get outside oneself."

As openness increases, political efficacy will increase, political interest will increase, political distrust will decrease, status quo orientation will decrease, and political participation will increase. Many of these are directly derived from previous findings. The openness-interest hypothesis follows from the likelihood that a more open person will be more likely to wish to gain information from the environment (recall that dogmatic people tend to be less well informed—tend to be resistant to seeking out or accepting information that does not fit with their preexisting beliefs). The trust-openness expectation follows from the finding that interpersonal trust is higher for open-minded people; it follows that trust of the larger political world might likewise increase.

As neuroticism increases for a respondent, political efficacy will decrease, political interest will decrease, political distrust will be unaffected, status quo orientation will be unchanged, and political participation will decrease. The distrust and status quo hypotheses are based on the finding that neuroticism goes with political alienation. The participation thesis arguably follows from this, since alienation often results in lessened traditional forms of political activity. Previous research on effects of depression (negative affect) suggests that interest (political apathy should be tied to less interest in politics) and participation ought to decrease (this would be expected, since depressed individuals are apathetic and feel as if they cannot control events handily).

The proper model for incorporating personality variables into predictions of political orientations and behavior must take into account standard accounts of the roots of political behavior and personality-based explanations. With the former, the Verba and Nie (1972) "socioeconomic model" is one of the best known and most well validated. This model can be illustrated thus:

$$\text{Socioeconomic status} \rightarrow \begin{matrix} \text{Civic} \\ \text{Orientations} \end{matrix} \rightarrow \begin{matrix} \text{Political} \\ \text{Participation} \end{matrix}$$

People higher in SES are more likely to exhibit "civic orientations" (civic duty, political interest, political efficacy, and the like). These orientations, in turn, lead to a greater predilection for taking part in political activities.

This model, however, does not consider personality variables. To accommodate this species of predictor, we assume that personality has an independent impact on both civic orientations and political participation, having an effect parallel to socioeconomic status. We assume that social forces are independent of personality. Personality has a direct impact on participation as well as an indirect effect through civic orientations—just as socioeconomic variables do. The model presented here guides data analysis later in this essay. The basic socioeconomic status variable that we use is education. Cutler (1977) has contended that, for older Americans, this is one of the most central predictors of political behavior. Hence, later, when we explicitly apply the above model, education serves as the SES control.

Methods. The 1987 Allegany County data provides the base for our exploration of the political effects of personality. The dependent variables are the ones that we have already described in previous parts of this book.

The independent variables are standard indices as well. Locus of control is arrived at by using a short form of the well known Rotter index. Extroversion, neuroticism, and openness are operationally defined by means of a shortened form of the NEO Inventory. This inventory has been validated for both younger and older samples.

Findings. First, we summarize factors associated with personality among the rural older Americans whom we are studying (See Table 3.4). Internal locus of control is greatest among the young-old, the educated, those with more social support and group ties, with fewer health and nutritional problems, and higher income. Extroversion and openness are quite similar to locus of control. However, with extroversion, being male also comes into play—increasing extroversion. With openness, being male and living in villages go with this personality characteristic. Those having higher scores on the neuroticism index are less educated, more isolated, sicker and less well nourished, poorer residents, and more likely to be female.

Table 3.4. Pearson's r: Correlates of Personality Variables.

	Internal locus of control	Extroversion	Openness	Neuroticism
Rural	.04	−.01	−.12**	−.01
Male	.06	.11**	.10**	−.11**
Age	−.25****	−.20****	−.23****	.02
Education	.24****	.17****	.31****	−.22****
Social support	.34****	.16****	.08*	−.23****
Group memberships	.32****	.17****	.18****	−24****
Health problems index	−.34****	−.17****	−.09**	.22****
Poor nutrition	−.23****	−.17****	−.09**	.13***
Income	.30****	.17***	.26****	−.21****

```
*    P < .10
**   P < .05
***  P < .01
****P < .001
```

Table 3.5 indicates the intercorrelations among the personality measures. We see that internal locus of control, extroversion, and openness are highly intercorrelated. Internal locus of control goes with less
neuroticism. Extroversion and openness are unrelated to neuroticism.
A first order test of the hypotheses is presented in Table 3.6; there is
considerable support for our expectations. Internal locus of control is
correlated with efficacy, interest, distrust, and participation as anticipated. It is also linked with two of the three measures of status quo
orientations as expected (locus of control is unrelated to conservatism). Extroversion is associated with efficacy, interest, distrust, and
participation as predicted. It is tied to only one of the three measures
of status quo support. Openness goes with efficacy, interest, distrust,
and participation as predicted. It is associated with two of the three
metrics of status quo support as anticipated. Finally, neuroticism. This
variable is correlated with efficacy, interest, and participation as called
for. In addition, it is related to greater distrust and less approval of
Reagan and lower odds of being Republican. Once more, this suggests
that neuroticism is part of a set of forces leading to greater alienation
from the system.

To ensure that zero-order correlations are not spurious, some controls are necessary. Here, we control for age, sex, education, and
group consciousness (the extent to which older Americans identify
themselves as part of a coherent group—operationalized as membership in some organization for older Americans [such as AARP]; on the
logic behind selecting this as a control variable, see Cutler, 1977).
Partial correlation coefficients, reported in Table 3.7, demonstrate that
most of the correlations obtained in Table 3.6 retain statistical signifi-

Table 3.5. Pearson's r: Correlation Matrix, Personality Variables.

	Internal locus of control	Extroversion	Openness	Neuroticism
Internal locus of control	—	.30****	.25****	−.39****
Extroversion		—	.32****	−.01
Openness			—	−.04
Neuroticism				—

*   P < .10
****P < .001

Table 3.6. Pearson's r: Dependent Variables with Personality Variables.

	Internal locus of control	*Extroversion*	*Openness*	*Neuroticism*
Political efficacy	.32****	.12**	.22****	−.32****
Political interest	.33****	.24****	.24****	−.31****
Conservative	−.02	.05	−.12**	.07
Approval of Ronald Reagan	.16***	.05	.01	−.16****
Republican	.09**	.11**	−.08*	−.15***
Political distrust	−.07*	−.17****	−.23****	.07*
Political participation	.30****	.21****	.31****	−.16****

*   P < .10
** P < .05
*** P < .01
****P < .001

cance. While correlations, overall, decline, the pattern of findings continues. That is, older Americans' personality characteristics seem to have an independent impact on their political orientations and behavior.

Finally, we return to test the manner in which personality affects political participation. This is a key dependent variable, since, as numerous studies show (e.g., Verba and Nie, 1972), participation affects political decision makers and even bureaucrats. Our assumptions about the causal ordering of variables are illustrated in the figure earlier in this paper. We operationalize the components of the model thus: SES is indicated by educational level; civic orientations are represented by a summed index—composed of efficacy and interest (a person gets one point if very efficacious and one point if interested in politics; a score of 2 stands for high civic orientation and a score of 0 for minimal level); personality is ascertained by the indices already discussed; political participation is the index previously used. Four separate path analyses were conducted, one for each of the personality measures. Figure 3.2 reproduces these.

We find that internal locus of control, extroversion, and openness have statistically significant direct paths to participation (the path coefficients represent the standardized regression coefficients, or betas, from stepwise multiple regression), as well as indirect paths

Table 3.7. Partial Correlation Coefficients: Dependent Variables by
Personality Variables (Controlling Education, Group Consciousness,
Sex, and Age), N = 338.

	Internal locus of control	Extroversion	Openness	Neuroticism
Political efficacy	.25****	.05	.12**	−.26****
Political interest	.23****	.16****	.13***	−.25****
Conservative	.04	.10**	−.05	.04
Approval of Ronald				
Reagan	.17****	.06	.02	−.15***
Republican	.11**	.12**	−.09**	−.13***
Political distrust	−.04	−.15***	−.23****	.04
Political				
participation	.17****	.10**	.16***	−.05

*   P < .10
**   P < .05
***   P < .10
****P < .001

through civic orientations—precisely as predicted earlier. While neuroticism is not directly linked with participation, against our expectations, it does have an indirect impact on political activities through
effects on civic orientations. In sum, internal locus of control, extroversion, and openness all work to enhance participation, whereas
neuroticism functions to depress levels of political activity.

Summary and discussion. Our findings support the contention that
individual personality differences among older Americans predict their
political orientations and actions; personality traits have an independent impact on our subjects' political behavior. To summarize, extroverted and open subjects and those with a sense of mastery over their
environments are more politically active. Those with an internal locus
of control tend to be more politically efficacious, interested, and status
quo oriented. The extroverted people are more politically interested,
status quo oriented, and less distrustful of the political system. More
open personalities are more efficacious and interested, less Republican, and less cynical about politics. Neurotic individuals tended to be
less efficacious and interested, and less supportive of the status quo.
These results, in the main, are supportive of our hypotheses.

Path analyses also show that personality factors have independent

Figure 3.2. Path Models: Predicting Political Participation, N = 355.

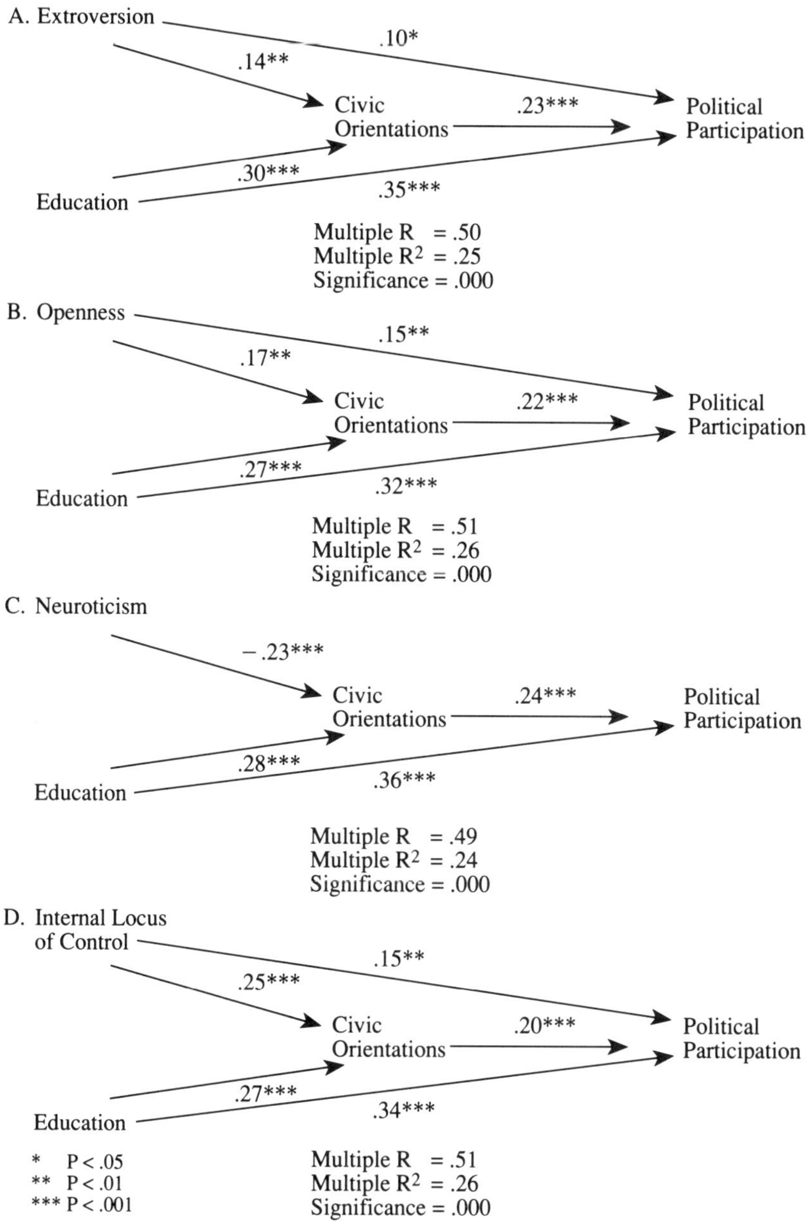

A. Extroversion

.10*

.14**

Civic Orientations .23*** Political Participation

.30***

.35***

Education

Multiple R = .50
Multiple R² = .25
Significance = .000

B. Openness

.15**

.17**

Civic Orientations .22*** Political Participation

.27***

.32***

Education

Multiple R = .51
Multiple R² = .26
Significance = .000

C. Neuroticism

− .23***

Civic Orientations .24*** Political Participation

.28***

.36***

Education

Multiple R = .49
Multiple R² = .24
Significance = .000

D. Internal Locus of Control

.15**

.25***

Civic Orientations .20*** Political Participation

.27***

.34***

Education

* P < .05	Multiple R = .51
** P < .01	Multiple R² = .26
*** P < .001	Significance = .000

impacts on basic political orientations and actions. All four personality variables have direct impacts on civic orientations; three have direct effects on political participation. While neuroticism does not have a direct path to political actions, it has an indirect impact through its influence on civic orientations.

Our analysis does have several shortcomings. The questionnaire was designed as part of a needs assessment study for a number of local agencies; hence, only truncated forms of the three NEO factors (openness, extroversion, neuroticism) were used to measure personality. The full scales should be used in future research. However, the fact that the truncated versions that we used still predict political orientations and participation suggest that the full scales would do at least as well. Thus, replication is called for.

There is also the question of external validity. Our findings were derived from a sample of rural elderly in one county within New York. This restricts somewhat any generalizations to the elderly in other venues. This also leads us to suggest replication on other samples of the rural elderly.

The results are important, we contend, because they shed additional light on the dynamics underlying the political beliefs and choices of rural older Americans. Some evidence suggests that rural elderly are at greater risk for mental disorders being experienced (Wagonfeld, Goldsmith, Stile, and Manderscheid, 1988), although there is a real gap in the literature on this question (e.g., see Human and Wasem, 1991; Scheidt, 1985). Thus, to the extent that the rural elderly may have somewhat greater psychological distress than their nonrural peers, our results may have some broader significance.

Those in our sample exhibiting neuroticism were less apt to take part in politics and be interested in the subject. This obviously reduces their political voice to some extent. Thus, greater mental dysfunction among rural elderly may make them less politically powerful. Thus, it does appears that personality traits represent one important set of factors helping to shape the political behavior of rural older Americans.

Life Satisfaction and Politics

Satisfaction with life is an important component of people's everyday lives. It is associated with affect (Campbell, 1981) and sense of personal competence (Campbell, Converse, and Rodgers, 1976). Campbell, Converse and Rodgers (1976) observe that it influences coping and adaptive behavior. Unhappiness with one's life can have political implications—if government is seen as an actor responsible for the source of displeasure (Brody and Sniderman, 1977; Sniderman and Brody, 1977). The focus of this research note is the effect of life satisfaction on political orientations and behavior among a sample of older Americans.

It seems sensible to assume that people's everyday lives will affect their perspectives toward the political world. Such routine events as health troubles, marriage, and retirement have all been found to have some relationship to people's political attitudes and behavior (e.g., Lupfer and Rosenberg, 1983; Peterson, 1990; Schwartz, 1976). Global satisfaction with one's life—the most important predictors of which include good family life, a satisfactory marriage, a sound financial situation, decent housing, a good job, inter alia (Campbell, Converse and Rodgers, 1976:85)—would seem likely to have some political effects.

In her intensive panel study of 21 Evanston residents, Graber found them (1984:52) "reasonably well-satisfied with life." She also discovered that the panelists were positive toward the political world. She suggests that (1984:52) "Their generally favorable outlook on politics may . . . spring from what is called 'stimulus generalization,' with general satisfaction casting a glow of good feeling over all aspects of life."

Life satisfaction is associated with greater self-confidence, self-esteem, interest in things and the belief that one controls one's own life (see Bradburn, 1969; Campbell, Converse and Rodgers, 1976). A number of these orientations are related to heightened political interest and political efficacy (e.g., see Milbrath and Goel, 1977). Through these intervening mechanisms, political participation would likely be increased (again, see Milbrath and Goel, 1977). Life satisfaction, indeed, has many of these predicted effects with Americans: those who are more satisfied participate more in politics, are more politically interested, follow the news regularly, are less alienated and more conservative (Peterson, 1991b).

What might be the impact of life satisfaction among older Americans? First, Campbell, Converse, and Rodgers (1976) observe that the young-old (65–74) and the old-old (75 and older) are the two age cohorts with the most elevated level of life satisfaction. Age, then, is not likely to be a potent mediating variable between life satisfaction and political orientations and behavior. Second, Cutler (1977) has asserted that two increasingly important predictors of political participation among the elderly are education and group consciousness. Education has been found to have an important role in individuals' life satisfaction (Campbell, Converse, and Rodgers [1976] find rather low satisfaction with different domains of life by the second highest educational category and rather high satisfaction by the lowest educational category); hence, this may well be an important variable mediating any linkages between life satisfaction and political orientations and behavior among older Americans.

Based upon the above consideration, we hypothesize that as life satisfaction among older Americans increases: (a) political efficacy will increase, (b) political interest will increase, (c) political participation will increase, and (d) satisfaction with the status quo will increase. Since there may be interactions with other variables influencing political orientations and behavior by older Americans, we also hypothesize that the relationships discovered in the preceding expectations will be maintained with the introduction of controls for education and group consciousness. This is, of course, a necessary companion hypothesis. If confirmed, this strengthens the case for life satisfaction as a shaper of political orientations and behavior. If disconfirmed, life satisfaction's role, obviously, is called into question.

Methods. Data were gathered as part of the 1987 needs assessment survey of the elderly in one rural county. The hypotheses raised above are tested on a very specific geographic sample. This clearly raises a question of external validity. Nonetheless, the respondents do provide data for a first-order test of seemingly important questions.

Life satisfaction is ascertained by responses on a five-point Likert-scale to the statement "How satisfied are you with your life as a whole these days?" (See Campbell, Converse, and Rodgers, 1976). There is some question about the validity of this measure (e.g., see Wilcox, 1980, 1981a, 1981b); nonetheless, this is the standard metric and represents life satisfaction in subsequent data analysis. Political participation is represented by a summed index of responses to four questions about extent of participation (whether or not individuals were registered to vote; whether or not individuals contributed to a political cause; how often individuals worked with others to solve a political problem; whether or not individuals had contacted a bureaucracy about some problem). Political interest is ascertained by respondent's indication about how often they follow politics and public affairs. Political efficacy is defined in terms of responses to two questions ("People like me don't have any say about what the government does"; "I don't think that public officials care much what people like me think"). Support for the status quo is indicated by conservative and Republican identification (whether rightly or wrongly, conservatives and Republicans are generally thought of as less oriented toward change), approval of former President Ronald Reagan (he was President at the time of the survey), and trust in the political system. Group consciousness is indirectly measured as membership in some organization for the aged—an imprecise indicator, but the best available from the questionnaire.

Findings. As would be expected (Campbell, Converse and Rodgers, 1976), there is a high level of life satisfaction. 54% of the respondents were very satisfied and 32% satisfied with their lives. Only 4% registered dissatisfaction.

Table 3.8 presents correlates of life satisfaction. We find that greater education, higher income, having roots in an area, owning a home, not facing transportation and housing problems, having group memberships, being healthy, and having a social support network all go with greater life satisfaction—exactly as one would guess.

Table 3.8. Pearson's Correlation Coefficients: Correlates of Life Satisfaction

	Life Satisfaction
Education	.16****
Female	.01
Age	.03
Income	.19****
Rural	.04
Married	.07*
Length of residence in area	.11**
Homeowner	.10**
Housing problems	−.24****
Transportation problems	−.25****
Regular church attendance	.12**
Group memberships	.20****
Health problems	−.29****
Nutritional problems	−.21****
Social support network	.34****

* $P < .10$
** $P < .05$
*** $P < .01$
****$P < .001$

Table 3.9 presents the relationships between life satisfaction and a series of basic political orientations and behavior. Basically, greater life satisfaction goes with more political efficacy, greater political interest, higher levels of political participation, higher approval ratings for former President Reagan, and higher likelihood of identifying as a Republican. There is no effect on ideology and trust.

However, we must control for possibly confounding factors. Hence, Table 3.9 also reports the standardized regression coefficients from listwise multiple regression analysis, controlling for education and group consciousness. With controls in place, life satisfaction is still associated with political efficacy and political interest. Its relationships with other variables, though, disappear.

One final test of the effects of life satisfaction is summarized in Figure 3.3. This depicts results of a path analysis with level of political participation as dependent variable. Assumptions of the model include: civic orientations (a variable combining individuals' level of political interest with level of political efficacy) affect political participation, as would group consciousness and education level. Findings reported above suggest that life satisfaction does not have an independent impact on participation with controls for education and group consciousness. Hence, we assume that there will be an indirect effect via its relationship with both efficacy and interest. Indeed, life satisfaction

Table 3.9. Multiple Regression: Life Satisfaction as a Predictor of Political Orientations and Behavior (controlling education and group consciousness).

| | *Life Satisfaction* | | |
	r	*Beta*	*N*
Political efficacy	.18****	.13**	350
Political interest	.23****	.17****	347
Political participation	.11**	.03	350
Conservative ideology	− .02	− .04	328
Approval of Ronald Regan	.11**	.09	328
Republican identification	.10**	.09	336
Political trust	.06	.03	350

* P < .10
** P < .05
*** P < .01
****P < .001

Figure 3.3. Path Model: Predicting Political Participation, N = 350.

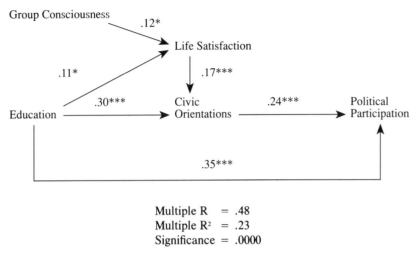

Group Consciousness

.12*

Life Satisfaction

.11* .17***

.30*** Civic .24*** Political
Education ——————→ Orientations ——————→ Participation

.35***

Multiple R = .48
Multiple R² = .23
Significance = .0000

* P < .05
***P < .001

has some impact on political activity via its effect on civic orientations; however, the impact is mild indeed. Other predictors are obviously more important.

Discussion. The findings of this study are rather easy to summarize. First, there is a pattern of correlation between life satisfaction, efficacy, and participation. The independent variable's impact is lessened considerably when controls are introduced. Nonetheless, some effects do remain. Finally, path analysis indicates that life satisfaction has an indirect link with participation mediated through civic orientations.

Essentially, the results suggest that one's day-to-day life (the end result of which is summarized by the satisfaction measure) has some tie to political participation. The magnitude of that effect is not great. However, as Wilcox points out, one would not expect there to be a remarkably powerful direct effect. In fact, he argues, political scientists ought to be more interested in distant background factors as these influence political orientations and behavior. At any rate, the findings here are that increasing satisfaction with a person's life—through intervening mechanisms—is associated with higher levels of participation.

There are some difficulties with this study. The one measure used to tap life satisfaction is only a summary metric. Furthermore, the sample serving as the data base here is composed of rural elderly from just one county in upstate New York. Hence, there is a question of external validity. However, the results are suggestive: one's quality of life may well have important effects on people's views of the political world.

Broader implications? Liang and Warfel (1983) report that those in urban areas are somewhat less satisfied with their lives, but the effects of place of residence are rather indirect. Analysis of the 1987 National Opinion Research Center General Social Survey data suggests that living in rural areas *per se* has little relationship to life satisfaction. These findings would indicate that life satisfaction as a factor in people's everyday lives probably has the same political effects in urban as well as rural areas. Thus, our findings may have somewhat more general applicability to the elderly than one might suppose. Indeed, results reported upon in this section are quite similar to those obtained when using the 1987 General Social Survey data base (Peterson and Somit, 1992), in that greater life satisfaction ultimately leads to higher levels of political participation.

References

Abramson, Paul R. 1983. *Political Attitudes in America*. San Francisco: W. H. Freeman and Company.

Agnello, T. J. 1973. Aging and the sense of political powerlessness. *Public Opinion Quarterly* 37: 251–259.

Barnes, Samuel H., Max Kaase, et al. 1979. *Political Action*. Beverly Hills: Sage.

Baumann, B. 1961. Diversities in conceptions of health and physical fitness. *Journal of Health and Social Behavior* 2: 39–46.

Booth, Alan and Susan Welch. 1976. Stress, health, and political participation. Presented at International Political Science Association meeting, Edinburgh.

Bradburn, N. M. 1969. *The Structure of Psychological Well-Being*. Chicago: Aldine.

Brody, Richard and Paul M. Sniderman. 1977. From life space to polling place. *British Journal of Political Science* 7: 337–360.

Brunswick, A. F. 1977. Indicators of health status in adolescents. In J. Elinson and A. E. Siegmann (eds.), *Socio-Medical Indicators*. Farmingdale, NY: Baywood Publishing Company.

Campbell, Angus. 1981. *The Sense of Well-Being in America*. New York: McGraw-Hill.

Campbell, Angus, Philip E. Converse, Warren E. Miller, and Donald E. Stokes. 1964. *The American Voter*. New York: John Wiley.

Campbell, Angus, Philip E. Converse, and Willard L. Rodgers. 1976. *The Quality of American Life*. New York: Russell Sage Foundation.

Campbell, Bruce A. 1979. *The American Electorate*. New York: Holt, Rinehart and Winston.

Caspi, Avshalom. 1987. Personality in the life course. *Journal of Personality and Social Psychology* 53: 1200–1213.

Costa, Paul T., Jr. and Robert R. McCrae. 1985. *The NEO Personality Inventory*. Odessa, Florida: Psychological Assessment Resources, Inc.

Costa, Paul T., Jr. and Robert R. McCrae. 1986. Personality stability and its implications for clinical psychology. *Clinical Psychology* 6: 407–423.

Costa, Paul T., Jr. 1988. Personality stability and the transitions and changes of adult life. APA Master lecture, Atlanta, Georgia.

Cutler, Neil E. 1977. Demographic, social-psychological, and political factors in the politics of aging. *American Political Science Review* 71: 1011–1025.

Cutler, Neil E. and John R. Schmidhauser. 1975. Age and political behavior. In Diana S. Woodruff and James E. Birren (eds.), *Aging*. New York: D. Van Nostrand.

DeVries, Walter and V. Lance Tarrance. 1972. *The Ticket-Splitter*. Grand Rapids: William Eerdmans Publishing.

Democracy is . . . 1991. Democracy is ageless. *AARPVoter* 5 (December): 4.

Elizabeth, Pamela and Steven A. Peterson. 1984. Decision theory, dogmatism, and politics. Presented at International Conference on Authoritarianism and Dogmatism, Potsdam, NY.

Erikson, Robert S., Norman R. Luttbeg, and Kent L. Tedin. 1991. *American Public Opinion*. New York: John Wiley & Sons, 4th edition.

Ferraro, Kenneth F. 1980. Self-ratings of health among the old and the old-old. *Journal of Health and Social Behavior* 21: 377–383.

Fillenbaum, G. G. 1979. Social context and self-assessments of health among the elderly. *Journal of Health and Social Behavior* 20: 45–51.

Fiske, Susan T., Donald R. Kinder, and W. Michael Larter. 1983. The novice and the expert. *Journal of Experimental Social Psychology* 19: 381–400.

Garrity, T. F. 1978. Factors influencing self-assessments of health. *Social Science and Medicine* 12: 77–81.

Gilmour, Robert S. and Robert B. Lamb. 1975. *Political Alienation in Contemporary America*. New York: St. Martin's Press.

Glenn, Norval D. and Ted Hefner. 1972. Further evidence on aging and party identification. *Public Opinion Quarterly* 36: 31–47.

Graber, Doris. 1983. *Processing the News*. New York: Longmans.

Greenstein, Fred I. 1969. *Personality and Politics*. Chicago: Markham.

Greenstein, Fred I. 1975. Personality and politics. In Fred I. Greenstein and Nelson W. Polsby (eds.), *Handbook of Political Science, Volume II: Micropolitical Theory*. Reading, Mass.: Addison-Wesley.

Hudson, Robert B. and Robert H. Binstock. 1976. Political systems and aging. In: Robert H. Binstock and Ethel Shanas (eds.), *Handbook of Aging and the Social Sciences*. New York: D. Van Nostrand.

Hudson, Robert B. and John M. Strate. 1985. Aging and political systems. In Robert H. Binstock and Ethel Shanas (eds.), *Handbook of Aging and the Social Sciences*. New York: Van Nostrand Reinhold, 2nd edition.

Hughes, Alan. 1975. *Psychology and the Political Experience*. Cambridge: Cambridge University Press.

Human, J. and Wasem, C. 1991. Rural mental health in America. *American Psychologist* 46: 232–239.

Idler, E. L. and S. Kasl. 1991. Health perceptions and survival. *Journal of Gerontology* 46: S55–S65.

Jacobs. Bruce. 1990. Aging and politics. In Robert H. Binstock and Linda K. George (eds.), *Handbook of Aging and the Social Sciences*. New York: Academic Press, 3rd edition.

Jennings, M. Kent and Gregory B. Markus. 1984. Political orientations over the long haul. *American Political Science Review* 78: 1000–1018.

Jennings, M. Kent and Gregory B. Markus. 1988. Political involvement in the later years. *American Journal of Political Science* 32: 382–316.

Kagan, Jerome. 1980. Perspectives on continuity. In Orville Brim, Jr. and Jerome Kagan (eds.), *Constancy and Change in Human Development*. Cambridge: Harvard University Press.

Kagan, Jerome. 1984. *The Nature of the Child*. New York: Basic Books.

Kaplan, G., V. Barell, and A. Lusky. 1988. Subjective state of health and survival in elderly adults. *Journal of Gerontology* 43: S114–S120.

Knutson, Jeanne N. 1973. Personality in the study of politics. In Jeanne N. Knutson (ed.), *Handbook of Political Psychology*. San Francisco: Jossey-Bass.

Kobassa, S. C. 1982. The hardy personality. In G. S. Sanders and J. Suls (eds.), *Social Psychology of Health and Illness*. Hillsdale, NJ: Lawrence Erlbaum Associates.

Liang, J. and B. L. Warfel. 1983. Urbanism and life satisfaction among the aged. *Journal of Gerontology* 38: 97–106.

Light, Larry. 1981. Democrats hoping to break traditional GOP loyalties of voters 65 and older. *Congressional Quarterly* 39: 2343–2346.

Lipset, Seymour Martin. 1960. *Political Man*. Garden City: Doubleday Anchor Books.

Longino, Charles F., Jr., Beth J. Soldo, and Kenneth G. Manton. 1990. Demography of aging in the United States. In Kenneth F. Ferraro (ed.), *Gerontology*. New York: Springer Publishing Co.

Lupfer, Michael and J. P. Rosenberg. 1983. Differences in adults' political orientations as a function of age. *Journal of Social Psychology* 119: 125–133.

McBride, Allen. 1980. Health and body image: effect on socialization. Presented at Midwest Political Science Association meeting, Chicago.

McCrae, Robert R. and Paul T. Costa, Jr. 1984. *Emerging Lives, Enduring Dispositions*. Boston: Little, Brown.

McCrae, Robert R. and Paul T. Costa, Jr. 1988. Age, personality, and the spontaneous self-concept. *Journal of Gerontology* 46: 5177–5185.

Milbrath, Lester W. and M. L. Goel. 1977. *Political Participation*. Chicago: Rand-McNally, 2nd edition.

Miller, Warren E. and Teresa Levitin. 1976. *Leadership & Change*. Cambridge: Winthrop Publishers.

Moss, Howard A. and Elizabeth J. Susman. 1980. Longitudinal study of personality development. In Orville G. Brim, Jr. and Jerome Kagan (eds.), *Constancy and Change in Human Development*. Cambridge: Harvard University Press.

Mussen, Paul and A. B. Wyszynski. 1952. Personality and political participation. *Human Relations* 5: 65–82.

Nie, Norman, Sidney Verba, and Jae-On Kim. 1974. Political participation and the life cycle. *Comparative Politics* 6: 319–340.

Norman, W. T. 1963. Toward an adequate taxonomy of personality attributes. *Journal of Abnormal and Social Psychology* 66: 574–583.

Peterson, Steven A. 1973. The effects of physiological variables upon student protest behavior. Presented at International Political Science Association meeting, Montreal.

Peterson, Steven A. 1974. Biological bases of student protest. Unpublished Ph. D. dissertation, State University of New York at Buffalo.

Peterson, Steven A. 1987a. Biology and political behavior. Presented at International Political Science Association Conference on Biopolitics, Warsaw, Poland.

Peterson, Steven A. 1987b. Biosocial predictors of older Americans' political participation. *Politics and the Life Sciences* 5: 246–251.

Peterson, Steven A. 1988. Health and the polity. Presented at International Political Science Association meeting, Washington, D. C.

Peterson, Steven A.1990. *Political Behavior: Patterns in Everyday Life*. Beverly Hills: Sage.

Peterson, Steven A. 1991a. Health of the polity. *Politics and the Life Sciences* 10: 65–68.

Peterson, Steven A. 1991b. 'No Te Preocupes, Se Feliz': Satisfaccion con la Vida y Politica. *Psicologia Politica* 3: 65–75.

Peterson, Steven A. and Albert Somit. 1978. Student protest: a biomedical perspective. *Journal of Higher Education* 3: 233–244.

Peterson, Steven A. and Albert Somit. 1990. Older Americans' health status and their political behavior. Presented at Animal Behavior Society meeting, Binghamton, NY.

Peterson, Steven A. and Albert Somit. 1992. Life satisfaction and politics among the elderly. *The Political Behavior of Older Americans*. New York: Garland Press (under contract).

Rokeach, Milton. 1960. *The Open and Closed Mind*. New York: Basic Books.

Rodin, Judith and Gail McAvay. 1992. Determinants of change in perceived health in a longitudinal study of older Americans. *Journal of Gerontology* 47: P373–P384.

Rowe, John W. and Robert L. Kahn. 1988. Human aging: usual and successful. *Science* 237: 143–149.

Sanders, G. S. 1982. Social comparison and perceptions of health and illness. In G. S. Sanders and J. Suls (eds.), *Social Psychology of Health and Illness*. Hillsdale, NJ: Lawrence Erlbaum Associates.

Scheidt, Rick J. 1985. The mental health of the aged in rural environments. In Raymond T. Coward and Gary R. Lee (eds.), *The Elderly in Rural Society*. New York: Springer Publishing Company.

Schubert, Glendon. 1983. Aging, conservatism, and political behavior. *Micropolitics* 3: 135–179.

Schwartz, David C. 1970. Perceptions of personal energy and the adoption of basic behavioral orientations to politics. Presented at International Political Science Association meeting, Munich.

Schwartz, David C. 1976a. The influence of health status on basic attitudes in an American political elite. Presented at International Political Science Association meeting, Edinburgh.

Schwartz, David C. 1976b. Somatic states and political behavior. In Albert Somit (ed.), *Biology and Politics*. Paris: Mouton.

Schwartz, David C. 1978. Health status, self-image, and political behavior in America's governmental elite. Presented at Western Political Science Association meeting, Los Angeles.

Schwartz, David C., Joseph Garrison, and James Alouf. 1975. Health, body images, and political socialization. In David C. Schwartz and Sandra Kenyon Schwartz (eds.), *New Directions in Political Socialization*. New York: Free Press.

Sherbourne, Cathy D. and Lisa S. Meredith. 1992. Quality of self-report data. *Journal of Gerontology* 47: s204–s211.

Smith, M. Brewster. 1972. A map for the analysis of personality and politics. In Samuel Kirkpatrick and Lawrence K. Pettit (eds.), *The Social Psychology of Political Life*. Belmont, CA: Duxbury Press.

Sniderman, Paul M. and Richard Brody. 1977. Coping: the ethic of self-reliance. *American Journal of Political Science* 21: 501–522.

Somit, Albert and Steven A. Peterson. 1990. The political behavior of the aged: What we know, what we don't know, and why? Presented at International Conference on the Future of Adult Life, Leeuwenhorst, The Netherlands.

Stone, William F. 1974. *The Psychology of Politics*. New York: The Free Press.

Stone, William F. 1980. The myth of left-wing authoritarianism. *Political Psychology* 2: 3–19.

Stone, William F. 1981. Political psychology: a Whig history. In Samuel L. Long (ed.), *The Handbook of Political Behavior*. New York: Plenum Press.

Strate, John M., Charles J. Parrish, Charles D. Elder, and Coit Ford III. 1989.

Life span civic development and voting participation. *American Political Science Review* 83: 443–464.

Sullivan, John L., James Piereson, and George E. Marcus. 1982. *Political Tolerance and American Democracy.* Chicago: University of Chicago Press.

Verba, Sidney and Norman H. Nie. 1972. *Participation in America.* New York: Harper and Row.

Wagonfeld, M. O., H. F. Goldsmith, D. Stiles, and R. W. Manderscheid. 1988. In-patient mental health services in metropolitan and non-metropolitan counties. *Journal of Rural Community Psychology* 9: 13–28.

Ware, J. E., Jr. 1986. The assessment of health status. In L. H. Aiken and David Mechanic (eds.), *Applications of Social Science to Clinical Medicine and Social Policy.* New Brunswick, NJ: Rutgers University Press.

Wilcox, Allen R. 1980. Need theory and political participation: toward an agenda. Presented at International Society of Political Psychology meeting, Boston.

Wilcox, Allen R. 1981a. Dissatisfaction with satisfaction. In Dennis Johnson (ed.), *The Measurement of Subjective Phenomena.* Washington, D. C.: Bureau of the Census.

Wilcox, Allen R. 1981b. Perceived quality of life and political activity. Presented at International Society of Political Psychology meeting, Mannheim, Federal Republic of Germany.

Williamson, John B., Linda Evans, and Lawrence A. Powell. 1982. *The Politics of Aging.* Springfield, IL: Charles C. Thomas.

Wolfinger, Raymond and Steven Rosenstone. 1980. *Who Votes?* New Haven: Yale University Press.

Wolinsky, Frederic D. 1980. *The Sociology of Health.* Boston: Little, Brown and Company.

Wolinsky, Frederic D. and Robert J. Johnson. 1992. Perceived health status and mortality among older men and women. *Journal of Gerontology* 47: S304–S312.

Chapter 4

Public Lives, Part II: Program Encounters of the Rural Elderly

Introduction

General Comments. It is by now a commonplace that government programs and their attendant bureaucracies offer Americans literally cradle-to-grave coverage. Barbara Nelson (1980) refers to people's use of programs as "invisible politics." She notes that, for instance, 78 million Americans voted in the 1972 presidential elections; in that same year, 52 million Americans applied for or received public benefits or services. She concludes that ". . . for ordinary citizens, political life is more and more characterized by a request for a check, not a trip to the polls" (p. 175). And this applies to older Americans as well.

Making contact with unelected public officials is also an important form of political participation—and is an action separate from using programs. Contact with bureaucrats has become a significant type of political behavior as bureaucratization increasingly describes American political society (e.g., Goodsell, 1981; Nachmias and Rosenbloom, 1980).

Krout notes the standard view that in rural areas there is (1986: 7) ". . . a lack of availability and accessibility of a wide range of services when compared to urban places." Furthermore, service delivery becomes more problematic with widely dispersed, relatively low density populations (see various essays in Binstock and George, 1990). Cost-effectiveness of delivering services declines, putting an additional strain on what is, in many rural counties, a rather poor tax base (for a general perspective on the importance of population density and tax base on service delivery, see Lewis and Anechiarico, 1981). Transportation systems are not as effective in rural as opposed to urban areas (*Old Age and Ruralism*, 1980). Thus, there are additional challenges facing rural elderly in terms of program usage and simply contacting public officials responsible for those programs.

This chapter focuses on several issues: (1) those factors shaping awareness of and use of programs designed to meet older Americans' needs; (2) variables that influence older Americans' satisfaction with programs; (3) an examination of contact with bureaucrats as political behavior. We apply our own variation of one standard model for explaining program use. We try to interpret our findings in terms of the different challenges facing those living in rural areas.

Predicting Program Awareness and Use

How do rural older Americans generally come to know of programs designed to help them? How do they come to use these programs? As more and more Americans enter the rural aged cohort, there will be greater demand for programs designed to assist elderly citizens. In this section, we begin by developing a model of those factors most apt to be associated with program usage. The bulk of this research has **not** been carried out on rural elderly (see Krout, 1983a for one significant exception). Thus, we survey two different literatures on those variables purported to be linked to program usage. Then, we apply the resultant model to our sample of rural elderly.

We explore the two questions posed at the outset with data gathered on the 1983 sample of rural elderly from upstate New York. This data set is used because of its somewhat more complete set of questions on overall program use and awareness as compared with the 1987 study. In later chapters, we use data from the 1987 study as well, since it had certain variables built in that go beyond the set of predictor variables available from the 1983 study. We develop a model to predict extent of program awareness and actual program use, based on literatures in gerontology and political science which examine correlates of program encounters. To this point, no research has drawn these separate lines of research together and tried to synthesize them. And certainly no one has applied the product of this union to rural elderly.

First, we consider those factors which have been found to shape the level of program awareness. This is an important task, since research by both gerontologists (e.g., Ward, 1977; Snider, 1980a) and political and policy scientists (Katz et al., 1975) indicates that awareness is one critical step in the process by which people come to actually use programs. Simply, knowing about programs increases the odds of using them.

Disciplinary Research

Gerontology. Ward et al. (1984) (and see Chapleski, 1989) find that extent of social ties is linked to greater awareness of programs. This, presumably, because these relationships provide a network of people who could have some knowledge about programs designed to meet the needs of a person; the person, then, would be informed by group members of such programs. On the other hand, though, program awareness actually declines with dependence on close family members and confidants for information. This may come about because these people provide substitutes for formal services to the elderly, and, hence, diminish the perceived need by people to seek out those formal services.

Education level has been found to enhance program awareness (Krout, 1983b; Snider, 1980b). Some research has implicated age as a factor associated with program awareness. The oldest-old (85 and over in age) were least aware of programs and the young-old (60–74) most aware (Peterson and Maiden, 1987; See also Snider, 1980a). Some evidence suggests that lower levels of awareness are manifest in rural as opposed to more urban areas (Snider, 1980a; Krout, 1988). Actual experience with programs is correlated with greater program awareness; that is, using, for instance, health services, makes people more aware of available health programs. Thus, program use itself has an educative function (Snider, 1980a; Chapleski, 1989). Those with greater reported incomes tend to be more aware of programs and the services which they offer (Snider, 1980a). Females tend to be more aware, as do those who are married (Krout, 1983a). Those with deficits in activities of daily living, blacks, and those with transportation problems seem to be less aware of programs (Chapleski, 1989). Finally, there is some evidence that need leads to greater awareness (Snider, 1980a).

Political Science. Research in political science has focused on awareness of programs by the general population. While this is a broader population than the aged, the perspective, nonetheless, provides suggestions about relevant predictor variables. Some work indicates that social networks provide one basis for becoming aware of programs

(B. Nelson, 1980). Another variable which would seem tied to awareness is need for services. Logically, one would expect that as need
increases for a person, that individual would begin a search procedure
to find out what programs could help to meet that need.

In the study of political behavior, one well-known correspondence
is between political involvement and political participation. One specific measure of political involvement is interest in politics—which is,
itself, tied to greater levels of information (Milbrath and Goel, 1977),
one type of which would be awareness of programs. Some evidence
suggests that greater interest in politics is associated with greater
program awareness (Peterson, 1987).

Another factor which could be related to program awareness is self-
confidence or a sense of personal "power." The political manifestation
of this is political efficacy, the belief that one can have an effect on
politics and public officials. Those with greater sense of control over
events are more likely to "take charge" and seek out information for
programs if they feel some need has to be met. Findings suggest that
while there is a reasonable zero-order relationship between political
efficacy and program awareness, that correlation disappears with the
introduction of statistical controls (Peterson, 1987).

Both political and policy scientists, on the one hand, and gerontologists, on the other, have tried to explain why people use programs.
Next, we survey both literatures to indicate the variables which are
deemed most important by each. Several models have been advanced;
we begin by noting a very common model emerging from research in
gerontology.

Theoretical Models

Gerontology. One model used by gerontologists to explain program
utilization (Andersen and Newman, 1973; Krout, Cutler, and Coward,
1990; Rabiner, 1992; Ward, 1977) is composed of three predictive
factors: (1) predisposing variables (those factors which exist prior to
the actual beginning of a need and which affect propensity to use
services); (2) enabling conditions (those which make services accessible and available to individuals who might wish to use them); (3) need
level (much of the literature focuses on use of health programs and
more narrowly refer to this as "illness factors"; however, it surely
seems more appropriate to speak to this as need for services, since the
model can then be generalized to other than just health program usage
[see, for instance, Ward, 1977]). Examples of predisposing factors are

demographic (age, sex, marital status, past problems), social structure (education, race, occupation, residential mobility, religion), and belief (attitudes toward using health services, knowledge about disease) variables. Enabling factors include family (income, having health insurance) and community (ratio of services to population, price of services, urban-rural nature of residence). The original formulation, as noted above, had the third determinant as illness level (although need level seems a more general and, hence, more useful term), including type of disability, symptoms, diagnoses, and general state of health.

Specific variables' effects have been explored. With greater age, for instance, some studies have suggested goes greater program use (Krout, 1983a); however, others find precisely the contrary (Peterson and Maiden, 1987). Those who are married have been found to have higher levels of utilization of programs (Krout, 1983a; but cf. Snider, 1980a). Income as predictor has led to a mixed bag of findings—sometimes tied to greater use and sometimes to less (cf. Krout, 1983a; Snider, 1980b; Ward, 1977). Access to transportation seems to enhance the extent of program use, largely because people find it easier to get to those programs which do not come to them (Krout, 1983a; Ward, 1977).

Unsurprisingly, program awareness is related to actual utilization (Snider, 1980a; Ward, 1977; Krout, 1983a, 1983b). Those with greater need have been found to make more extensive use of programs (Snider, 1980a; Rabiner, 1992). One study suggests that greater political activity goes with increased use (Ward, 1977). Rural background is normally—but not always—found to be tied to less usage (cf. Ward, 1977; Krout, 1983a; G. Nelson, 1980). Females have been found to use programs more than males (Krout, 1983b). Research indicates that group memberships are often associated with greater program use (Krout, 1983b; and see Ward et al., 1984). Finally, there is some hint that greater life satisfaction is linked with more programs being used (Krout, 1983b; Snider, 1980a). Less education may lead to greater program use (Krout, 1983a, 1983b). Living alone is associated with greater use (Snider, 1980a).

An entirely different set of factors associated with program usage is an individual's values and beliefs. Moen (1978) finds rather low program utilization among those elderly with needs. She suggests that this may be the result of values which discourage accepting government help. However, there are few data available to establish the accuracy of this hypothesis (and see Ward, 1977:63).

Finally, bureaucratic variables can affect people's use of programs.

The paperwork often faced by clients may deter their desire to use some service. So, too, may the impersonality with which agencies process clients (See Krout, 1983b).

Political Science. A set of independent variables has been advanced to explain contacts with bureaucracy. First, there is need. Vedlitz et al. (1980) find that greater need is associated with increased contacting (and see Hirlinger, 1992). Second, awareness of programs. Katz et al. (1975) have observed that awareness of programs is tied to increased use of program services (See also Sharp, 1982).

A third set of variables is based on the view that citizen bureaucratic encounters are a form of political participation, and, hence, will be predicted by the "socioeconomic model" (Verba and Nie, 1972). Here, SES affects civic orientations (e.g., political efficacy and involvement) which, in their turn, increase the odds of participating in politics. Some studies do find that socioeconomic status is tied to contact behavior (Lehnen, 1976; Sharp, 1982; Vedlitz and Veblen, 1980. But cf. Verba and Nie, 1972).

Fourth, social involvement. Brown (1982) has discovered that the number of individuals' group memberships is linked to a greater number of contacts. Finally, political participation. Zuckerman and West (1985) analyze Verba/Nie/Kim's seven-nation data (Verba, Nie and Kim, 1978) and find that respondents most active in partisan political activities are more apt to contact public officials about particularized problems (see also Jones, 1981). The logic? Zuckerman and West say (1985:130):

Political connections, especially to parties, emerge as the major structural basis for overcoming the limitations on political action imposed by poverty and ignorance. Efforts to increased citizen demands on governments grow and are most effective when linked to political parties.

A number of interactive models have emerged. Jones et al. (1977) developed a "parabolic model" which incorporates need and awareness. They claim that as the social well-being of areas increases, need declines whereas program awareness increases. Their prediction is that contact would be greatest in the middle ranges of well-being, since there would be both a moderate level of need and reasonable awareness. Data from Detroit provide some support for the parabolic model, although this finding has not been successfully replicated (see Vedlitz et al., 1980; Sharp, 1982, 1984; Brown, 1982; Thomas, 1982).

Thomas (1982) has advanced a second interactive model—"clientele participation"—which represents a synthesis of the needs approach and the socioeconomic model. Using individual level data from Cincinnati, he argues that (1982:518):

> . . . citizen-initiated contacts with government agencies will be a function primarily of perceived needs, an individual's instrumental concerns, and secondarily of the socioeconomic model, presumably the general political attitudes and information that also affect traditional forms of political participation.

If he is correct, then standard predictors of political participation—as well as need—should both have important roles in predicting level of contact.

Then, there is Sharp's variation on Thomas' model. She finds that another type of interaction between need and SES predicts contacting behavior. Data from a sample of Kansas City residents provides support for her "contingent need" hypothesis (1984:661; but cf. Peterson, 1986):

> Where perceived need for services is high, socioeconomic status is of negligible importance in predicting contacting behavior; but where perceived need is low, socioeconomic status is a significant predictor of contacting behavior.

Discussion and Synthesis. While existing literature features a number of explanatory models, there are problems which must be addressed. Much gerontology research refers to the Andersen-Newman "enabling-predisposing-illness [need] factors" model. However, there are some real difficulties with this approach. First off, explained variation in studies using this perspective is often quite modest.

Second, results applying the Andersen-Newman model are often conflicting. The survey of literature on earlier pages of this chapter illustrates (and see Krout, 1983b). Third, some argue that social-psychological variables (such as life satisfaction) ought to be considered more centrally than is normally done with the Andersen model (Krout, 1983b).

Fourth, variables within each of the three "factors" seem like a lumping together of apples and oranges. Predisposing factors include demographic, social, and belief variables. The first two seem very much related; age, sex, marital status, education, etc. are all social resources that influence individuals' transactions with their environment. Advantages accrue to those with certain resources (such as more education, being married, being younger). Beliefs would appear to be on a quite distinct dimension, although values and beliefs will be associated in predictable ways with social resources. Enabling factors such as income seem more closely allied to the social resources noted above than with other "enabling factors" like program characteristics and rules and geography.

While the Andersen framework has been useful as a way of organizing the literature (and this is very important indeed), it does not seem to be the best way of trying to explain people's use of programs. The political/policy science literature is in worse shape. There are a series of single predictor or two variable models, as noted above; there has been no full multivariate analysis to tease out the different variables' roles to this point (although see Peterson, 1987). Explained variation is generally quite modest. Finally, results obtained to this point in a variety of studies are conflicting (e.g., on Thomas' two-factor model, see Thomas, 1982; Sharp, 1984; Peterson, 1986).

We have tried to synthesize the various findings, literatures, and theoretical perspectives. Below is a five component model by which program utilization might be predicted. Previous literature on program encounters in both gerontology and political science suggests several categories of predictive variables:

(1) Personal resources: This represents the individuals's personal, internal resources for carrying out transactions with the larger environment. This includes psychological characteristics such as a sense of mastery over the environment (or, in technical terms, internal locus of control) and political efficacy (sense that one can affect politics). Another personal resource would be information level; as one has more information, one is more likely to know about programs and how to get assistance. Previous research suggests that internal locus of control, political efficacy, political interest and overall life satisfaction ought to enhance program awareness and increase the extent of contacts (e.g., see Peterson, 1987; Sharp, 1982; Snider, 1980a). Just so, then, older people with greater personal resources ought to be characterized as having higher levels of program awareness and use.

(2) Social resources: These include education level, income, group ties, social support networks, age, marital status, access to transportation, urban vs. rural residence, political party-oriented involvement. Each of these aspects of one's social being has some effect on program use or awareness—although the exact impact of each is not clear from

existing research (e.g., cf. Ward et al., 1984; Ward, 1977; Krout, 1983a, 1983b; Brown, 1982; Zuckerman and West, 1985; Peterson, 1986, 1987). These social resources, in turn, should have an influence on individuals' personal resources. For instance, more education is tied to greater sense of mastery over the larger environment. This introduces an indirect effect of social resources on program encounters. In the end, greater social resources are expected to covary with greater program awareness and use.

(3) Need: This seems straightforward enough. From research in both political science and gerontology, there is a tie between greater need and greater program use. One would also expect that need would drive people to find out about programs that could help them; in this manner, need would elevate awareness. Although the literature has some contradictory findings, in general, it does suggest that greater need should go with greater awareness and use (Ward, 1977; Krout, 1983b; Rabiner, 1992; Snider, 1980; Thomas, 1982).

(4) Program-related factors: Some programs are harder to use than others and are harder to know about. Examples of the former include programs the use of which carries some stigma, such as means-tested programs. Other programs are small and poorly publicized; these would lead to less awareness as well as lower levels of use (Nelson, 1980). Still other programs involve cost-sharing which might dissuade potential users. Finally, paperwork may be odious to possible users and, hence, discourage them. One would expect that more visible and more accessible programs would lead to greater program awareness and use (and see Ward, 1977; Krout, 1983b).

(5) Values and beliefs: Some people are resistant to using public programs, on the grounds that they should take care of their own problems. On ideological or value bases, they are loath to use programs (e.g., see Briggs, 1986; Krout, 1983a; Ward, 1977; Moen, 1978). Regrettably, the 1983 data base does not include good measures of values or beliefs, so their impact is assessed on the basis of an admittedly crude indicator.

At the risk of greatly oversimplifying a complex reality, an arrow diagram depicting the nexus of relationships can be constructed. Figure 4.1 outlines one possible model. Social resources and need level are the two background variables. They affect the intervening variables (personal resources, values, program awareness) as well as program use. This is a "situational" model, in that social situations and conditions of need are seen as shaping values and personal resources more than the latter influence need and social resources. Situations are seen

Figure 4.1. Arrow Diagram: Predicted Pattern of Relationships with Program Awareness and Use.

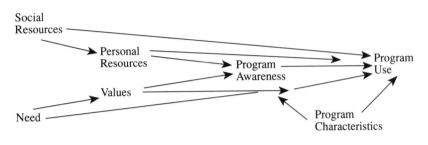

as affecting people's values and their self-perceptions and personality characteristics (e.g., see Kagan, 1984; Somit and Peterson, 1987). Program characteristics are exogenous—from outside the individual—and affect both program awareness and use.

Methods. The sample, as mentioned before, is the 456 older Americans from Allegany County interviewed in 1983. Dependent variables include both program awareness and program use. Each respondent was asked how many of 28 programs listed he or she was aware of. Program awareness is simply the number of programs people claim that they know about (see Table 4.1 for a listing). Program use is indicated by individuals' counts of how many of those 28 programs in Table 4.1 that they actually used.

The independent variables are generally quite straightforward. First are the social resources. Rural residence is measured as a person saying that he or she lives on a farm or in the country. Sex is simply a self-report of respondents' gender. Group membership is a summed index, telling one the extent of social ties possessed by a respondent (membership in a senior citizens' club, membership in an organization for older Americans, membership in any other organizations), social support addresses the extent to which individuals have networks to assist them (it is also a summed index, indicating how many of the following supports each person reported having: most of one's friends nearby, having someone to call in case of an emergency, not being lonely). Age is trichotomized: young-old (60 to 74), old-old (75 to 84), oldest-old (85 and over). Education is registered simply as highest level of education attained, in number of years of education. Being married is ascertained by a simple self-report of marital status. Mobility is still another summed index, designed to indicate the access to transporta-

Table 4.1. Older Citizens and Their Program Encounters, N = 456.

Program	Awareness N	Awareness %	Use N	Use %	Satisfaction N	Satisfaction %
OFA nutrition	381	84	60	13	53	88
Mobile Meals	412	90	24	5	15	63
Friendly Visitors	201	44	4	1	3	75
Telephone reassurance	207	45	4	1	3	60
Household Assistant	304	67	17	4	15	88
Homemaker	310	68	11	2	8	73
Home Health Aides	287	63	16	4	14	88
Public Health Nurses	404	89	39	9	34	87
Houghton Van	130	29	10	2	10	100
Community Express Inc.	207	45	16	4	14	88
Housing Action Corp.	198	43	22	5	16	73
Green Thumb	329	72	16	4	12	75
Legal Services	256	56	4	1	4	100
Hope and Cope	28	6	0	0	—	—
Medical Transportation	285	63	11	2	10	91
Elderhostel	117	26	3	1	3	100
Tax Assistance	281	62	21	5	20	95
Dollar Stretcher	301	66	115	25	101	88
Cooking Class	191	42	2	0	2	100
Employment Program	223	49	1	0	0	0
Share-A-House	253	56	2	0	2	100
Cheese Distribution	419	92	230	50	220	96
Senior Citizens' Clubs	408	90	141	31	132	94
Blind Association	315	69	10	2	9	90
American Cancer Society	428	94	52	11	45	87
Human Service Satellite	90	20	0	0	—	—
Information and Referral	154	34	14	3	12	86
Recreation	244	54	18	4	15	83

tion available to respondents (specific items are being able to get where desired by public transportation, having a car in working condition in the household, and not reporting any problems with transportation). Party-oriented participation is an index of what seems to be partisan activities. People got one point if they were registered to vote and another if they reported actually voting in the 1982 Congressional elections.

Personal resources are a second general category of independent variable. Political interest indicates the extent to which a person reports following politics and public affairs; political efficacy represents the individual's sense that he or she can have an effect on public officials. Locus of control is measured by an abbreviated form of the familiar Rotter index; it suggests the level of mastery that a person feels he or she has over life. Life satisfaction is a metric asking how satisfied (or dissatisfied) people are with their lives in general.

Need is a summed index indicating the number of areas (nine in all, including nutrition, health care, housing, finances, etc.) in which a person admits to having some need. An indirect measure of values and beliefs was created to represent an individualistic orientation, in which a person would resist using programs on the grounds that he or she should take care of problems on his or her own. One question in the needs assessment instrument asked people why they did not use Food Stamps. Two responses were "don't want it" and "don't like program." Individuals who answered with either of these responses were counted as having individualistic values; the logic is straightforward—many people who disapprove of Food Stamps or who would refuse to use them—even if eligible—do not believe in the propriety of accepting government help. This is a crude measure and it was selected post hoc. At the time the questionnaire was being constructed, we did not realize the potential importance of adding a values indicator, and the standardized survey instrument did not include any other questions even remotely related to values and beliefs. Finally, the surrogate measure of program characteristics is program awareness, which has already been described.

Findings. Program use is the central dependent variable. There is a reasonable degree of variation with it; the range is from zero to ten programs reported used. The mean number utilized is 1.9 and the median is 2. Program awareness is an important intervening variable. The range of programs individuals claim to be aware of runs from zero to (not very credibly) all 28. The mean number reported known about is 16 and the median is 16.5.

Table 4.2 reports on the Pearson's correlation coefficients between the different sets of predictor variables and program awareness and use. For program awareness, social resources enhance number of programs aware of, as do personal resources. Need, however, is rather strongly related inversely—against expectations. More specifically, the strongest correlates of program awareness are, in descending order, group memberships, education, political interest, party-oriented activities, internal locus of control, political efficacy, transportation, and

Table 4.2. Pearson's r: Correlates of Program Awareness and Use,
N = 433.

	Program Awareness	Program Use
Social Resources		
Rural	−.06	−.08*
Group memberships	.37****	.27****
Social support	.05	.16****
Age	−.30****	.05
Education	.36****	−.03
Party-oriented activities	.24****	.02
Married	.15****	−.21****
Transportation	.16****	−.06
Male	.01	−.16****
Personal Resources		
Political interest	.26****	.06
Political efficacy	.17****	−.09**
Internal locus of control	.20****	−.09**
Life satisfaction	.05	.03
Need	−.22****	.18****
Individualistic values	−.01	−.01
Program Awareness	—	.14****

*   P < .10
**   P < .05
*** P < .01
****P < .001

being married. Greater age and increased needs go along with lowered program awareness. Values are not linked to awareness.

Table 4.2 also provides information on correlates of program usage. Certain social resources, need, and program awareness are all linked with greater use; personal resources, on the other hand, are modestly and negatively related to utilization level—against expectations. Strongest correlates of increased use are, in order, group memberships, need, social support, and program awareness. Associated with less use are being married, being male, political efficacy, internal locus of control, and being from the countryside rather than from a village.

Individualistic values are unrelated to use. Before trying to make sense of these results, though, multivariate analysis must be undertaken. Table 4.3 reports findings from a listwise multiple regression analysis. Here, the independent variables "compete" with one another to see which retain the greatest impact while taking into account the

Table 4.3. Standardized Regression Coefficients (Betas): Predicting Program Awareness and Program Use, N = 433.

	Program Awareness	*Program Use*
Social Resources		
Rural	−.04	−.04
Group memberships	.34****	.33****
Social support	−.11**	−.08
Age	−.25****	.02
Education	.23****	−.15***
Party-oriented activities	−.02	.04
Married	.03	−.19****
Transportation	.00	.05
Male	.00	−.07
Personal Resources		
Political interest	.08*	.08
Political efficacy	.00	−.08
Internal locus of control	.05	−.03
Life satisfaction	−.07	.07
Need	−.04	.24****
Individualistic values	−.04	.03
Program Awareness	—	.14****
Multiple R	.57	.46
Unadjusted Multiple R²	.33	.21
Adjusted Multiple R²	.30	.18
Significance	.000	.000

*   P < .10
**   P < .05
*** P < .01
****P < .001

effects of all the other independent variables. With program awareness as dependent, need drops out as a predictor. Among the personal resources, only political interest continues to be associated with greater awareness. Finally, group memberships and education, qua social resources, continue to bear strong relationships with awareness. Greater age and more social support (against expectations) covary with less awareness. The explained variation is fairly high (30% when adjusted; 32% unadjusted).

Strongest predictors of program use are group memberships, need, and program awareness. Factors which are tied to less use are being married and greater education. Explained variation is modest but reasonable.

Finally, we return to the arrow diagram noted in Figure 4.1. Data at hand provide the ability to test how well this model describes the data. From each of the five categories of predictor, the one with the strongest beta from Table 3 was selected for inclusion in a regression-based pathlike analysis. Group membership represents social resources; political interest stands for personal resources. Need, individualistic values, and program awareness are the three other variables entered. The results appear in Figure 4.2. The Multiple R is .27 and the model explains a modest 7% of the variation in program utilization.

Individualistic values have no impact on awareness or use. Program awareness, group memberships, and need all have direct paths to

---

Figure 4.2. Arrow Diagram: Predicting Program Use, N = 451.

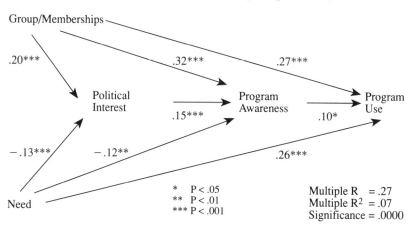

program use. Political interest has an indirect path through its effects on program awareness. Both group membership and need have a one-step-removed path to use through their effects on awareness and a two-steps-removed impact through political interest. Group membership (a social resource) has the greatest total effect on use, followed by need level. In this statistical exercise, unlike that summarized in Table 4.3, need is linked with lowered awareness. Overall, the empirically-derived model is fairly close to that which was predicted in Figure 4.1. The major difference is the lack of impact by individualistic values (which can easily be explained by the unsatisfactory post hoc operationalization of that variable).

Summary. First, a brief summary of findings is in order. Older citizens' program awareness and use vary a great deal across the rural sample examined in this essay. Correlational analysis tells us that social resources are generally associated in predicted directions with both awareness and use. The strongest social predictors of awareness include group memberships, education, young-old age status, and party-oriented political behavior. The greatest social influences on program use are number of group memberships and marital status (married persons are less likely to use programs). Personal resources, with no statistical controls in place, are related to greater awareness but (marginally) less use of programs. Need is tied to less awareness and greater use. Individualistic values, as measured here, have no impact on either awareness or use. Program awareness itself is linked with elevated usage of programs.

However, when multivariate analysis is undertaken, the personal resources are greatly diminished as effective predictors of either awareness or use. Need is no longer tied to awareness, although it retains its relationship with higher levels of use. Individualistic values continue to be unrelated to either dependent variable. Program awareness is tied to greater use of programs by respondents. Social resources tend to hold up well as effective predictors of both awareness and usage.

Regression-based pathlike analysis further clarifies the network of relationships among the various categories of independent variable. Values drop out of the arrow diagram which summarizes results. However, the other categories bear associations with one another and with awareness and use as anticipated.

The one category which performs most poorly is values and beliefs. This is not difficult to understand solely on measurement grounds; the metric for individualistic beliefs is very indirect. The rationale for the role of values and beliefs is very strong. Future research should certainly utilize more direct indicators of this (probably) important influence on program use (e.g., see Conover and Feldman, 1984; Feldman, 1983). Indeed, our 1987 sample explicitly built in more direct measures, and their effects are reported upon in later chapters.

This section began with the questions of how best to explain what factors shape older Americans' program encounters—their awareness of and use of programs. We have argued that a synthesis of efforts in political science and gerontology is one promising approach to addressing these riddles. While the five factor model which we have developed shows some promise (once again, taking into account the likely measurement-based failure of the values/beliefs variable), questions remain.

First, and most obviously, much variation remains unexplained— especially for extent of program use. A part of this is doubtless due to the well-known problem of indicator unreliability in survey research. This is hardly likely to be the only explanation, however. The model elaborated upon in this paper implies a longitudinal process—with factors affecting awareness and, through awareness, actual use; we also expected direct, unmediated effects of some of these variables on use. The data are based on a one-shot survey, though, not on a panel study. It would take a panel study to examine the over-time process by which people come to be aware of and use programs. This "compression" of the data may weaken the empirical relationships that emerge from statistical analysis (for instance, it is hard to believe that the Pearson's r between awareness and use is only .14). And, it is possible that researchers have simply missed important variables that shape persons' program encounters.

Second, even if the explained variation is not great, it is also not bad by the normal standards of social science. This suggests that there is some value to our approach. Certainly, it would seem worthwhile to continue exploring the roots of people's program-oriented activities. The literature, to this point, has not been pulled together particularly well. Separate research industries in political/policy science and gerontology have not been linked at all by researchers—even though both literatures are quite visible in their respective disciplines. Whether or not the effort that we have outlined in the preceding pages proves in the end to be useful, the drawing together of hitherto separate research agendas across disciplines is itself a valuable enterprise.

In the final analysis, these results also testify to the additional obstacles facing rural elderly in access to programs designed to help them. Programs appear to be less coordinated in rural areas; adequate transportation services are spottier; there is less money usually available to develop programs and generate successful outreach (*Old Age and Ruralism*, 1980). Simply geographical factors make it more difficult to deliver services to the elderly in rural counties (once more, note Lewis and Anechiarico, 1981).

Program Satisfaction

The starting point for this discussion is the observation that most people are very satisfied by their bureaucratic encounters (e.g., Goodsell, 1981b; Jacob, 1972; Katz et al., 1975; Nelson, 1981). While there are some questions about how satisfaction is actually measured (Gutek, 1978; Nelson, 1981), evaluations are so positive using a wide array of metrics that one has to conclude that people are generally pretty happy with services rendered by programs. Furthermore, older Americans seem especially satisfied with services (Goodsell, 1981a). Nonetheless, satisfaction is hardly universal. A series of hypotheses has been advanced over time as to what factors actually influence levels of satisfaction.

Goodsell (1981a) observes that "greater efficaciousness"—most notably among older Americans—enhances satisfaction, although he provides no direct evidence of this. England and Levenbach (1991) contend that basic political orientations (ideology, for instance) are important factors predicting satisfaction with local government services. In his study of citizens' contacts with bureaucracy in three Milwaukee neighborhoods, Herbert Jacob (1972) finds that the poor and working-class recipients are most positive about programs (see also Nelson, 1981). Hence, we would expect satisfaction to increase as a person's socioeconomic status goes down. Nelson (1981) suggests more globally—and contrary to Goodsell—that a client's dependence on a program and an accompanying sense of helplessness will lead to greater satisfaction. Many clients have great need for programs; they appreciate any help that they can get—they have little choice in the matter.

Finally a study well over fifty years old—carried out by Gabriel Almond and Harold Lasswell (1934)—posits additional variables that might affect program satisfaction. Their dependent variable in this venerable study is termed aggressiveness, but this actually appears to be a measure of program dissatisfaction. Clients on public relief were defined as aggressive if they went to the complaint desk and made demands, complaints, threats, and so on. This seems to be, on its face, an indicator of dissatisfaction (and see Katz et al., 1975). Their observations suggest several correlates of dissatisfaction, including greater experience with programs, greater political activity levels, greater sense of alienation and powerlessness (Contra Nelson), and younger age.

The literature on program satisfaction is tangled. We find contradictory expectations, as with the sense of personal empowerment. Nelson claims that dependence and powerlessness breed satisfaction; Goodsell notes that personal efficacy elevates satisfaction; Almond and Lasswell contend that powerlessness and alienation go with dissatisfaction.

Methods. Once more, we use the 1983 data set. Table 4.1 reports upon the level of satisfaction for each program reportedly used by respondents. There is considerable variation here, with some programs receiving very high approval by respondents and others getting measurably less approbation. To study the effects of a variety of predictors, we created a summed index of program satisfaction. For each respondent, number of programs used was tallied. Then, number of programs satisfied with was counted. Finally, we divided number satisfied with by total number of programs used. Overall, from Table 4.1, it is abundantly clear that older Americans in Allegany County were generally very pleased with the programs that they used. Since variation is not great with the index described in the preceding sentences, we also created a dichotomized form of program satisfaction, with a person receiving a score of 1 if satisfied with all programs used and 0 if dissatisfied with even a single program used. The independent variables have already been discussed above in more detail. We use level of education, political efficacy, internal locus of control, need, political participation, number of programs used, and age.

Results. Table 4.4 reports the findings from statistical analysis. Pearson's correlations show that few of the expectations described above are met; indeed, results are disappointing. For both measures, greater political efficacy goes with more satisfaction (as Goodsell speculates) and program use and age with dissatisfaction (as Almond and Lasswell reported over half a century ago). Table 4.4 also depicts the betas from listwise multiple regression analysis. The key influence—far and away—is the sheer number of programs used. That is, the more programs you use, the greater the odds of disliking one. The only other variable with any impact at all is age. Younger-old are more satisfied than their elders with programs used. The explained variation

Table 4.4. Multiple Regression: Predicting Program Satisfaction,
N = 325.

	Program Satisfaction		*Dichotomous Measure of Program Satisfaction*	
	r	*Beta*	*r*	*Beta*
Education	.01	−.01	.00	−.02
Political efficacy	.08	.07	.10**	.07
Internal locus of control	.02	−.01	.01	−.03
Need	−.03	.00	−.06	−.01
Political participation	−.04	−.03	−.04	−.01
Number of programs used	−.31****	−.30****	−.47****	−.46****
Age	−.11**	−.10*	−.09**	−.08*

*   P < .10
**   P < .05
*** P < .01
****P < .001

is very modest for the "pure" measure of satisfaction; it is somewhat greater for the dichotomous form of the dependent variable.

Explaining Bureaucratic Contacts

A series of independent variables has been advanced to explain contacts with bureaucracy. In our theoretical discussion much earlier in this chapter, we noted several of these emerging from the political science literature—our primary focus in this section. These include need (Vedlitz et al., 1980), program awareness (Katz et al., 1975), "socioeconomic model" variables, such as education and civic orientations (such as political interest and efficacy) (Verba and Nie, 1972; Lehnen, 1976; Sharp, 1982; Vedlitz and Veblen, 1980), social involvement (Brown, 1982), and political participation (Zuckerman and West, 1985).

Several interactive models, as discussed previously, have also emerged, such as the Jones et al. (1977) "parabolic model," the Thomas (1982) "clientele participation" model, and Sharp's "contingent need" hypothesis (Sharp, 1984). These interactive models, while advances over the single variable efforts at explaining bureaucratic encounters, only deal with two variables at a time. As summarized above, though, the literature has explored five predictors. No single study conducts a multivariate analysis taking into account all of these in trying to explain bureaucratic contacts. Before proceeding further, though, we must more clearly define what we mean by bureaucratic contacts as opposed to using programs administered by bureaucracies.

Nelson (1981) has made the basic point that individuals interact with or have contact with agencies which deliver services in a number of different ways (see also Lewis and Anechiarico, 1981; Percy and Scott, 1985). For conceptual purposes, one might begin by dividing citizen contacts with government agencies into "inputs" and "outtakes" (for more detail, see Peterson, 1986). Input behavior represents an individual's effort to get some government agency to respond to a particular problem (e.g., a missed garbage pickup). The citizen is an active participant, trying to get government to react. From the agency's point of view, such requests result in "demand processing"—receiving, channeling, and answering demands made of it (Percy and Scott, 1985). Much of the extant literature seems to address this species of citizen-government interaction (e.g., Sharp, 1982, 1984; Brown, 1982)—and this is what we refer to as bureaucratic contact in the paragraphs above.

The second type of citizen contact seems more akin to what Milbrath defines as outtakes, individuals' extractions from the political system (Milbrath and Goel, 1977). People are clients of programs and/or are receiving ongoing services. Recipients are often passive and dependent on the service provider (e.g., see Lewis and Anechiarico, 1981; Nelson, 1984). This is the focus, of course, of the bulk of the chapter up to this point.

While the same individual may engage in both types of contact, this is not necessarily the case. The two types of encounters are conceptually separate (although, in practice, there may be a blurring of the lines between input and outtake behaviors, although we note in passing that the Pearson's correlation between our measure of bureaucratic contact and programs used is only .05—surely suggesting that these two phenomena are not the same). In the literature on bureaucratic contact, though, that distinction has not been clearly drawn. We do so here.

Using 16 studies as a data base, we find the following patterns (those studies include Brown, 1982; Hirlinger, 1992; Lehnen, 1976; Mladenka, 1977; Katz et al., 1975; Jones et al., 1977; Jones, 1981; Jacob, 1972; Sharp 1982, 1984; Thomas, 1982; Vedlitz et al., 1980; Vedlitz and Veblen, 1980; Verba and Nie, 1972; Shin and Everson, 1980; Zuckerman and West, 1985):

(1) SES: Of 13 studies including a measure of SES, 9 report at least a mild positive relationship with contact.
(2) Need: Of 7 studies including an index of need, 5 report some positive association with contact.
(3) Awareness: Of 3 studies using a metric for awareness, 3 find a positive relationship with contact.
(4) Social involvement: The one study including such a variable finds a positive association with contact.
(5) Political participation: Of 3 studies asking about extent of participation 3 find a positive relationship with contact.
(6) Civic orientations: Of 4 studies including some index of civic orientation, 2 suggest a positive tie with contact.

Although there is conflict in the findings, then, there is also some support for the purported role of each of the independent variables dominant in the literature. However, there has been no multivariate analysis designed to get at the relative impact of each of the predictors. In the analysis to follow, we explore that issue.

Methods. Once more, the 1983 sample of 456 older Americans residing in Allegany County, New York is the data base for this analysis. Bureaucratic contact was measured as follows: a question asking how often (never, once, a few times, many times) each respondent had contacted a bureaucrat or bureaucracy about some problem. Independent variables are political efficacy, political interest, political participation (e.g., being registered to vote, having voted in 1982 elections, joining with others in the community to advance some political interest), years of education, group membership, measures of need (e.g., difficulties with transportation, housing, health, financial resources, etc.), and program awareness, the extent of an individual's recognition of the 28 programs listed in Table 4.1.

Findings. The modal response for number of bureaucratic contacts is none, as is the median. The standard deviation is 1.0. There is not a great deal of variation; rather few respondents initiate many contacts.

In some ways this is not surprising, since bureaucratic contacting is an active form of political participation.

Table 4.5 tells of the network of Pearson's rs between the independent variables and bureaucratic contact. All are associated with contacts—but need is linked in an inverse direction, opposite expectations. The strongest correlates are political participation, education, program awareness, and political efficacy.

Multivariate analysis is called for to discern the relative contribution of each of the seven predictors. In Table 4.5, the betas from listwise multiple regression appear. The best predictors of bureaucratic contacting (in descending order) are political participation, program awareness, political efficacy, and need (the last in a direction contrary to expectations). Only modest variation is explained.

To obtain a more precise sense of the processes at work, we conducted a path analysis. Figure 4.3 presents the complicated web of interactions shaping extent of contacting (stepwise multiple regression is used, with a cutoff point of $p < .05$ for including a path). Political participation, program awareness, and political efficacy all have direct paths to this variable. Indirect effects abound; program awareness, efficacy, interest, education, need, and group membership all manifest such influence.

Quickly to summarize basic findings: In order of magnitude, Pearson's correlation coefficients with strong relationships to contacting

Table 4.5. Multiple Regression: Predicting Bureaucratic Contacting, N = 456.

	Bureaucratic Contacts	
	r	*Beta*
Group membership	.12***	−.07
Program awareness	.21****	.11**
Need	−.15****	−.08*
Education	.26****	.08
Political interest	.18****	.04
Political efficacy	.20****	.08*
Political participation	.34****	.26****

*   P < .10
**   P < .05
***   P < .01
****P < .001

Figure 4.3.   Arrow Diagram: Predicting Bureaucratic Contacts,
N = 456.

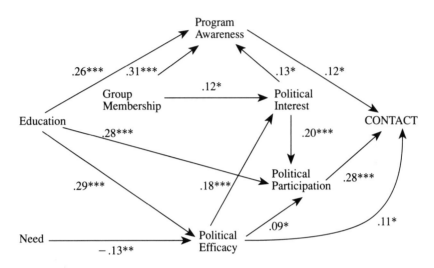

Multiple R= .38; Multiple R² = .14; Significance = 0.0.
*p < .05; **p < .01; ***p < .001.

are political participation, education, program awareness, political efficacy, political interest, group membership, and (inversely) need. Multivariate analysis indicates that participation, awareness, efficacy, and (inversely) need are the most important predictors. 15% of the variation is explained. Path analysis reveals a complex web of interactions, with three predictors—participation, awareness, and efficacy—having direct paths to bureaucratic contacts.

Discussion. One final observation. Overall, the literature on contacting bureaucrats is interesting and features many clever efforts to explain the phenomenon. However, at least in the studies reported upon here, rather little variation seems to be explained by the major variables thus far identified in this corpus. The results described herein indicate a serious challenge facing those working within this area. There are many pieces of a jigsaw puzzle lying about in the literature. These have not yet been put together in a way that solves that puzzle. There is enough unexplained variation that it seems clear that further work is needed to discover those factors crucial for shaping contact with programs by older Americans.

However, this is an important issue to explore further. Evidence makes it clear that contacting bureaucrats or agencies can lead to their responding to the demands placed upon them (e.g., Greene, 1991; Jones, 1977). Thus, citizen participation can make a difference—but only if people contact bureaucracy in the first instance. Two key predictors among our sample for explaining contacting behavior are program awareness and political participation. We have seen elsewhere some of the obstacles facing rural elderly in becoming aware of programs in the first place, even though some difficulties, such as fragmentation and poor coordination, have been increasingly addressed in recent years (Alter, 1988). This dynamic would reduce the odds of contacting bureaucracy.

However, we also know (see Table 3.1) that rural elderly are somewhat more apt to participate in politics and contact bureaucrats. This suggests that the rural ambience serves to increase, in the final analysis, the probability of older citizens contacting bureaucracies about their own unique problems. Perhaps this is due to the greater closeness between citizens and their public servants. Verba and Nie (1972), after all, have concluded that Americans living outside of the metropolis are more prone to participate, presumably because of the smaller scale of government. Hence, rural elderly may have a greater opportunity to generate responsiveness from bureaucracy, partially as a result of their participation in the political realm.

References

Almond, Gabriel and Harold D. Lasswell. 1934. Aggressive behavior by clients toward public relief administration. *American Political Science Review* 28: 643–655.

Alter, Catherine Foster. 1988. The changing structure of elderly service delivery systems. *The Gerontologist* 28: 91–98.

Andersen, Ronald and John F. Newman. 1973. Societal and individual determinants of medical care utilization in the United States. *Milbank Memorial Fund Quarterly* 51: 95–124.

Binstock, Robert and Linda George (eds.). 1990. *Handbook of Aging and the Social Sciences*. New York: Academic Press, 3rd edition.

Briggs, David. 1986. Study cites pride of the elderly for low use of food programs. *The Buffalo News* December 18: B–16.

Brown, Steven D. 1982. The explanation of particularized contacting. *Urban Affairs Quarterly* 18: 217–234.

Chapleski, Elizabeth E. 1989. Determinants of knowledge of services among the elderly. *The Gerontologist* 29: 539–545.

Conover, Pamela Johnston and Stanley Feldman. 1984. How people organize the political world: a schematic model. *American Journal of Political Science* 28: 95–126.

Cutler, Neil E. 1977. Demographic, social-psychological and political factors in the politics of aging. *American Political Science Review* 71: 1011–1025.

England, David E. and F. David Levenbach. 1991. A causal model of citizen satisfaction with local government services. Presented at American Political Science Association meeting, Washington, D. C.

Feldman, Stanley. 1983. Economic individualism and American public opinion. *American Politics Quarterly* 11: 3–30.

Goodsell, Charles T. 1981a. The contented older client of bureaucracy. *International Journal of Aging and Human Development* 14: 1–9.

Goodsell, Charles T. 1981b. Looking once again at human service bureaucracy. *Journal of Politics* 43: 763–778.

Greene, Kenneth R. 1991. Administrators' receptivity to citizen contacts. Presented at Northeastern Political Science Association meeting, Philadelphia.

Gutek, B. A. 1978. Strategies for studying client satisfaction. *Journal of Social Issues* 34: 44–56.

Hirlinger, Michael W. 1992. Citizen-initiated contacting of local government officials. *Journal of Politics* 54: 553–564.

Jacob, Herbert. 1972. Contact with government agencies. *Midwest Journal of Political Science* 16: 123–146.

Jones, Bryan. 1981. Party and bureaucracy. *American Political Science Review* 75: 688–700.

Jones, Bryan, Saadia R. Greenberg, Clifford Kaufman, and Joseph Drew. 1977. Bureaucratic response to citizen-initiated contacts. *American Political Science Review* 72: 148–165.

Kagan, Jerome. 1984. *The Nature of the Child.* New York: Basic Books.

Katz, Daniel, Barbara A. Gutek, Robert C. Kahn, and Eugenia Barton. 1975. *Bureaucratic Encounters.* Ann Arbor: Institute for Social Research.

Krout, John A. 1983a. Correlates of service utilization among the rural elderly. *The Gerontologist* 23: 500–504.

Krout, John A. 1983b. Knowledge and use of services by the elderly. *International Journal of Aging and Human Development* 17: 153–167.

Krout, John A. 1988. Community size differences in service awareness among elderly adults. *Journal of Gerontology* 43: 528–530.

Krout, John A., Stephen J. Cutler, and Raymond T. Coward. 1990. Correlates of senior center participation. *The Gerontologist* 30: 72–79.

Lehnen, Robert G. 1976. *American Institutions, Political Opinion, and Public Policy.* Hinsdale, IL: Dryden Press.

Lewis, E. and F. Anechiarico. 1981. *Urban America*. New York: Holt, Rinehart and Winston.

Maiden, Robert, Thomas A. Leitko, and Steven A. Peterson. 1984. Rural elderly. Presented at Gerontological Society of America, San Antonio, Texas.

Milbrath, Lester W. and M. L. Goel. 1977. *Political Participation*. Chicago: Rand-McNally, 2nd edition.

Mladenka, Kenneth R. 1977. Citizen demand and bureaucratic response. *Urban Affairs Quarterly* 12: 273–290.

Moen, Elizabeth. 1978. The reluctance of the elderly to accept services. *Social Problems* 25: 293–303.

Nachmias, K. R. and D. H. Rosenbloom. 1980. *Bureaucratic Government USA*. New York: St. Martin's.

Nelson, Barbara J. 1980. Help-seeking from public authorities. *Policy Sciences* 12: 175–192.

Nelson, Barbara J. 1981. Client evaluations of social programs. In Charles T. Goodsell (ed.), *The Public Encounter*. Bloomington, Indiana: Indiana University Press.

Nelson, Barbara J. 1984. Women's poverty and women's citizenship. *Signs* 10: 209–230.

Nelson, Gary. 1980. Social services to the urban and rural aged. *The Gerontologist* 20: 200–207.

Old Age and . . . 1980. *Old Age and Ruralism . . . A Case of Double Jeopardy*. Albany, NY: New York Senate Research Service.

Percy, S. L. and E. J. Scott. 1985. *Demand Processing and Performance in Public Service Agencies*. University: University of Alabama Press.

Peterson, Steven A. 1986. Close encounters of the bureaucratic kind. *American Journal of Political Science* 30: 347–356.

Peterson, Steven A. 1987. Older citizens' program encounters. *Journal of Applied Gerontology* 6: 39–52.

Rabiner, Donna J. 1992. The relationship between program participation, use of formal in-home care, and satisfaction with care in an elderly population. *The Gerontologist* 32: 805–812.

Sharp, Elaine B. 1982. Citizen-initiated contacting of government officials and socioeconomic status. *American Political Science Review* 76: 109–115.

Sharp, Elaine B. 1984. Citizen-demand making in the urban context. *American Political Science Review* 28: 654–670.

Shin, D. and David H. Everson. 1980. Participation in the Verba-Nie modes in three middle-sized cities. Presented at Midwest Political Science Association meeting, Chicago.

Snider, Earle L. 1980a. Awareness and use of health services by the elderly. *Medical Care* 18: 1177–1182.

Snider, Earle L. 1980b. Factors influencing health service knowledge among the elderly. *Journal of Health and Social Behavior*. 21: 371–377.

Somit, Albert and Steven A. Peterson. 1987. The primacy principle: a biosocial critique. *International Political Science Review* 8: 205–214.

Thomas, John Clayton. 1982. Citizen-initiated contacts with government agencies. *American Journal of Political Science* 26: 504–522.

Vedlitz, Arnold, James A. Dyer, and Roger Durand. 1980. Citizen contacts with local governments. *American Journal of Political Science* 24: 50–67.

Vedlitz, Arnold and Eric P. Veblen. 1980. Voting and contacting. *Urban Affairs Quarterly* 16: 31–48.

Verba, Sidney and Norman H. Nie. 1972. *Participation in America*. New York: Harper and Row.

Verba Sidney, Norman H. Nie, and Jae-On Kim. 1978. *Participation and Political Equality*. Cambridge: Cambridge University Press.

Ward, Russell A. 1977. Services for older people. *Journal of Health and Social Behavior* 18: 61–70.

Ward, Russell A., Susan R. Sherman, and Mark LaGory. 1984. Informal networks and knowledge of services for older persons. *Journal of Gerontology* 39: 216–223.

Zuckerman, Alan S. and Darrell M. West. 1985. The political bases of citizen contacting. *American Political Science Review* 79: 117–131.

Chapter 5

Case Studies:
Demographics and the Elderly

Introduction

The oldest-old are expected to more than double in number in the next 20 years (Rosenwaike, 1985). Given their unique needs (and see Bould, Sanborn, and Reif, 1989) our research reported upon below has important implications for governmental agencies responsible for the delivery of services and programs aimed at the well-being of the aged. Between 1960 and 1980, the oldest-old increased in numbers by 141% and now make up the fastest growing segment of the American population (Longino, 1988). One analyst notes that (Longino, 1988: 515) ". . . the sheer number of persons 85 years of age and over is now substantial enough to have a major impact on the health care and social service systems." It is noteworthy that almost half of the oldest-old have some significant disability (Longino, 1988).

What about those in rural areas? Bould, Sanborn, and Reif say that (1989: 48): "While 23% of the oldest old live in rural areas, rural residence poses particularly difficult problems for cost-effective program development." Making the current situation more challenging is that the rural oldest old are poorer than their nonrural peers and face greater difficulties in transportation.

In the future, the oldest-old will probably face fewer non-medical problems in their everyday lives. Serow and Sly note that (1988: 154): "These cohorts of future oldest-old will be better educated and will probably have more in the way of financial resources than did their predecessors. . .[T]he lot of future oldest-old cohorts, through that of 2020, will be superior to that of the present and immediate past."

While some have argued that the average life expectancy is not likely to move much beyond 85 (Olshansky, Carnes, and Cassel, 1990), that would still mean many more oldest-old than we have today. Will the oldest-old be very frail, with a rapid increase in morbidity coming at the end of their life span (Kramer, 1980; Olshansky, Carnes, and Cassell, 1990), thus taxing health care and social service agencies? Or will those attaining oldest-old status be able to experience good quality of life, as others have suggested, with a compression of ills coming at the very end of their life spans (Fries, 1980; and see the even more optimistic view in Rogers, Rogers, and Belanger, 1990; Rothenberg, Lentzner, and Parker, 1991)? Either way, there will be demands on service providers, although the burden will vary greatly depending on which scenario is manifest. It is incumbent upon researchers to ascertain those factors shaping the oldest-old's program-related behavior. This may be especially true for rural oldest-old, who have fewer programs available to help them and who may have more trouble gaining access to such programs that do exist.

Extant research suggests that the oldest-old are a unique population, distinct from those who have recently entered elderly status—the 60 to 70 year olds. The oldest-old have a disproportionate sex ratio— there is a much greater ratio of females to males than with any other age category (Suzman and Riley, 1985). They are considerably more likely to be living in an institution, less likely to be married and more likely to be impoverished and to have lower educational attainment (Suzman and Riley, 1985). Although the young-old have experienced recent gains in income, this is not as apparent among the oldest-old (Moon and Sawhill, 1985; Preston 1984a, 1984b). The differentiation among the elderly population has become so marked that it is no longer wise to treat everyone over the age of 60 as if they were a single aggregate, as was once commonly done (Suzman and Riley, 1985). One in four of the oldest-old is institutionalized; among the noninstitutionalized oldest-old, some 43 percent are dependent upon the help of another to function in activities of daily living, although the other 57 percent declared themselves free of any limitations and are independent (Feller, 1983).

Krout (1990) finds a curvilinear relationship between age and usage of social programs, with the young old (60–74) and oldest-old (85 and up) being least likely to utilize these. The need to appreciate age differentiation is especially true today when social service programs are being considered for substantial change and restructuring. Although the oldest-old are one of the fastest growing segments in the American population, little is known about their social and economic needs, their awareness of social programs or their use of social services (e.g. see New York State Office for the Aging, 1986). The first part of this chapter assesses the social, economic, and health needs of the oldest-old (over the age 85) as compared to the old-old (75–84) and the young-old (60–74) in a rural county in upstate New York.

We also consider the extent to which those needs are being met. In isolating the needs of the oldest-old, we look at an array of factors that might predict program usage, such as program awareness, involvement or participation in groups, level of need, years of education, sense of control over his or her life. We find that although the oldest-old have the greatest social and economic need, they are least likely—as compared to younger elderly—to actually use programs. Since the oldest-old are going to increase in numbers, our findings have important implications for governmental agencies responsible for the delivery of services and programs aimed at the well-being of the aged.

The second part of this chapter focuses on elderly females. This is a most significant group to consider since demographic data tell us that there are far more older females than there are older males in the United States—women live longer than men and, hence, come to be overrepresented in the ranks of the elderly. The implications for government programs are profound, since greater age is associated with diminished capacities for independent functioning and a corresponding greater need for assistance (Fowles, 1983).

Some have gone so far as to claim that the problems of old age are really the problems of females (Butler, 1980; Maiden, Leitko, and Peterson, 1984). Note that the oldest-old, discussed above, are largely females. Minkler and Stone (1985), indeed, argue that there is a "triple jeopardy among the elderly—being old, poor, and female." The three characteristics appear to cluster together.

Studies suggest that older females have more difficulties than their male counterparts. Older females are more likely to be widows and living alone and facing loneliness (Lammers, 1983; Lowy, 1985; Block et al., 1986). They have more problems with their finances than males—just making ends meet. Warlick has noted that government transfer programs (1983:46) ". . . exacerbate this differential, worsening the economic circumstances of aged women relative to men." A large part of this is the result of Social Security's treatment of older women who have been dependents throughout much of their potential career lives. Lammers has argued that, among the age cohort 75 years of age and older (1983:7), ". . . needs for income maintenance and health care go up sharply for individuals older than 75 and for persons living alone (which disproportionately includes elderly women)." Older women, since they are less likely to drive an automobile, have more difficulties getting around and locating adequate transportation (Krout, 1986). As one result of this pattern of greater needs experienced by older females, the Federal Council on Aging has proposed targeting social service programs more toward those with the kinds of problems faced disproportionately by older females. Thus, there is little question that older women face many challenges and that special efforts are warranted to address these needs.

Furthermore, Barbara Nelson has argued that much of women's public lives—aside from traditional types of political activities, such as voting—(1984:209) ". . . remains unchronicled and undervalued. . . ." While women are much more likely to be clients of welfare programs than males, there has been little explicit effort to explore these program encounters in any detail. The second part of this chapter explores one specific feature of older women's public lives—those factors shaping older females' program encounters (awareness of and use of programs). This is just one small part of the research program advocated by Nelson.

Finally, we consider the effects of "rurality," differences in place of residence within a rural area, more specifically, residing in the country versus living in a village. This can be a significant issue, since those living in the country are even less likely to have access to social services and health care facilities.

The third part of this chapter, then, explores the impact of place of residence within a rural county on older Americans' lives. We divide respondents to our 1987 survey into two groups—those living in the country or on farms versus those living in small towns and villages. We compare these two groups on such factors as program use and contacts with bureaucracy, personality, and other elements of a person's public life.

The Oldest-Old

Some studies have examined the array of factors which predict program usage, as we note in Chapter 4. However, no investigation has examined it from the perspective of the oldest-old. As we recounted in Chapter 4, program awareness was associated with greater education level, more group memberships, political interest, and a sense of the individual being able to control his or her own life (called internal locus of control). Factors linked to greater program usage included need level, program awareness, and being involved in groups. Those with more education were somewhat less likely to use programs. Another study performed in a small city in western New York reported additional findings (Krout, 1983). This investigation found that program use tended to be greater for the elderly who were unmarried, had less education, had more sick days, used their car less, and had less contact with their children.

We have already noted that the oldest-old have the lowest education levels. From other studies of the more general population, we know that education is related to greater awareness of programs; program awareness, in turn, leads to greater actual use of programs. Since the oldest-old have the lowest education levels, we believe that they would have the least amount of program awareness and program usage while having the greatest economic and social needs.

To examine these issues, we use the 1983 Allegany County data base. The key independent variables are generally familiar and straightforward. Group membership is ascertained by a summed index of three items: membership in social organizations, membership in an organization for the aged, and membership in a senior citizens' club. The basic measure of socioeconomic status is educational level. Internal locus of control is an abbreviated version of the Rotter index, and measures the extent to which people believe that they control their own lives. Age is indicated as follows: 1 = 60 to 74 years old; 2 = 75–84 years old; 3 = 85 and over. 259 respondents were 60 to 74; 147 were 75 to 84; 50 were 85 and older (the oldest-old). Need is figured by counting the number of different areas (nutrition, social needs, disability, health, transportation, activities and hobbies, legal problems, housing, and finances) in which people say they have some need. The majority of the respondents indicated either none or just one need. However, 45% of those interviewed said that they had more than one need (the most common needs, in order, have to do with health, personal disabilities, and transportation).

Findings. First, we report on how overall conditions of life and program awareness and use vary by age group. Table 5.1 summarizes these findings. The statistical technique used is one way analysis of variance. Essentially, the average scores of each variable are calculated for each of the three age groups. Then, these means are compared to see if any differences among the age groups are statistically significant. The table clearly shows many differences across the age groups.

Table 5.1. One Way Analysis of Variance: Life Conditions By Age, N = 456.

	Mean			*1-tail*	
	60–74	*75–84*	*85 +*	*F*	*P*
Education	11.6	10.8	10.3	5.9	.002
Mobility	2.7	2.6	2.3	6.3	.001
Group memberships	1.9	1.8	1.5	2.0	.140
Positive Affect	3.2	2.9	2.3	8.8	.000
Negative Affect	1.3	1.2	1.4	0.7	.242
Life Satisfaction*	0.7	0.9	0.8	2.7	.036
Number of physical infirmities	0.2	0.5	1.3	49.7	.000
Poor nutrition	0.2	0.2	0.5	2.2	.057
Number of personal disabilities	0.9	1.6	3.5	34.8	.000
Income**	17.9	14.6	12.2	5.1	.004
Memory problems***	1.5	1.4	1.3	2.9	.027
Need level Internal locus of control	5.5	4.8	4.0	14.4	.000
Number of programs aware of	17.5	15.9	10.0	31.4	.000
Number of programs used	1.8	2.2	1.6	2.7	.035

*   The higher the score, the lower the satisfaction
**   17.9 = $8000 per year; 14.6 = $7200 per year; 12.2 = $5300 per year
***The lower the score, the more the memory problems

Since our primary focus is the oldest-old, we summarize our findings for them.

The oldest-old, briefly, have the lowest educational level, the least ability to get around (much of which is the result of lack of transportation), less positive views toward themselves and the world, the greatest number of physical infirmities and personal disabilities (deficits in activities of daily living), poorer nutrition, less income, more troubles remembering things, much greater need and a lower sense of control over their lives.

With respect to existing programs, they are least aware of programs and use programs the least. This, despite the fact that we have already seen that they have, far and away, the greatest level of need.

Table 5.2 summarizes the extent to which age, group memberships, education, need level, and internal locus of control have an effect on program awareness. The average number of programs which individuals claim that they are aware of is 16.18. The statistical technique used to examine the relative impact of the different independent variables is multiple classification analysis.

Table 5.2. Multiple Classification Analysis: Predicting Program Awareness, N = 451.

Grand Mean = 16.18

	Category	N	Unadjusted Deviation	Eta	Adjusted Deviation	1-Tail Beta	P
Age	1	256	1.27		0.96		
	2	145	−0.12		0.06		
	3	50	−6.15	0.35	−5.07	0.28	.000
Group memberships	1	160	−2.65		−1.82		
	2	137	0.72		0.65		
	3	154	2.11	0.32	1.31	0.21	.000
Education	1	68	−3.83		−2.33		
	2	141	−1.29		−1.03		
	3	102	0.53		0.28		
	4	140	2.77	0.35	1.97	0.24	.000
Need	0	133	1.94		0.51		
	1	117	0.12		−0.21		
	2	95	−0.49		0.19		
	3	106	−2.13	0.23	−0.57	0.06	.269
Internal locus of control	1	161	−1.51		−0.51		
	2	171	−0.03		0.03		
	3	119	2.09	0.21	0.65	0.07	.149
Multiple R							.527
Multiple R^2							.278

The "unadjusted deviation" refers to the difference from the grand mean (16.18) of each category of each variable. For age, being in the first category (60 to 74) leads to being aware, on average, of 16.18 + 1.29 programs, or 17.47 in all. The 75 to 84 year old group is aware of 16.18−0.14, or 16.04, programs. The oldest-old are aware, on the average, of 16.18−6.15 or 10.03, programs. This is another way of saying that the oldest-old are least aware of existing programs. The "eta" figure can be interpreted as a type of correlation coefficient, with larger numbers representing a closer relationship between two variables. The data tell us that the more the group memberships, the higher the education, the less the need, and the greater the person's sense of control over events, then the greater the level of program awareness.

Table 5.2 also speaks of the impact of each of the five predictors on awareness while taking into account the effects of the other four. The "beta" refers to the strength of any variable's relationship with program awareness while controlling the effects of the four other variables. The "adjusted deviation" is the distance from the mean for each category of any variable while taking into account all of the other variables. This provides information about the independent impact of each variable. For instance, being 60 to 74 years old is tied to 16.18 + 0.99, 17.15, programs aware of when group membership, education, need, and locus of control are accounted for. Being 75 to 84 is, on the average, related to being aware of 16.20 programs when controlling for the other variables; being oldest-old (85 and over) is associated with knowing about 11.05 programs. The beta of 0.29 (with P level, or significance level, of .000) tells us that there is still a significant effect of age after all other variables considered here are accounted for.

Likewise, group memberships and education level continue to retain a strong independent impact on being aware of different programs when impacts of the other variables are considered. Need level and locus of control do not have much of an impact when all other factors are taken into account. The Multiple R^2 figure indicates that about 28% of the variation in program awareness is explained by these five predictor variables together. In short, age, group memberships, and education are the key shapers of extent of program awareness.

Table 5.3 also reports a multiple classification analysis, this time with number of programs used as the dependent variable. The overall average (grand mean) of number of programs used per person is 1.90. Predictors are age, group memberships, education, locus of control, level of need, and program awareness. The overall prediction of program use is not quite as good as with program awareness. The Multiple R^2 of .185 says that about 19% of the variation in respondents' program usage is explained by the six predictor variables together.

Table 5.3 shows that the variables with the greatest independent impact (according to the size of the betas and significance levels) on actual number of programs used are group memberships, need, and program awareness. As each of the three increases, so, too, does

Table 5.3. Multiple Classification Analysis: Predicting Number of Programs Used, N = 451.

Grand Mean = 1.90

	Category	N	Unadjusted Deviation	Eta	Adjusted Deviation	1-tail Beta	P
Oldest	1	256	−0.11		−0.05		
	2	145	0.30		0.20		
	3	50	−0.28	0.12	−0.34	0.09	.064
Group memberships	1	160	−0.53		−0.56		
	2	137	−0.17		−0.24		
	3	154	0.69	0.29	0.79	0.32	.000
Need	0	133	−0.35		−0.51		
	1	117	−0.36		−0.40		
	2	95	0.42		0.48		
	3	106	0.47	0.22	0.65	0.28	.000
Number of programs aware of	1	143	−0.36		−0.37		
	2	171	0.01		−0.02		
	3	119	−0.13	0.05	0.00	0.01	.484
Education	1	68	0.07		0.24		
	2	141	0.13		0.20		
	3	102	−0.17		−0.08		
	4	140	−0.05	0.06	−0.26	0.11	.064
Multiple R							.433
Multiple R^2							.188

program usage. Internal locus of control has no effect at all. Both education and age group are marginally tied to program utilization. Note the relationship between age and program use. The "adjusted deviations" tell us that the young-old use programs a little less than average (this makes sense, since they have less need). The second category (75 to 84) uses more than the average number of programs. However, the oldest-old, with the greatest level of need, as we have already emphasized, use fewer programs than either of the two younger groups.

Discussion. The central question of this portion of the chapter has been the effect of age on program awareness and program use. The data make it clear that the oldest-old are least aware of programs and use these the least of any among the elderly—despite their greater needs. The oldest-old are also the least educated, the least involved in groups, and have the lowest sense of control over their lives ("internal locus of control"). We can summarize our basic findings about program awareness and use as follows:

(1) Those least aware of programs are the oldest-old, those without group ties, and those with a low level of education. Ironically, those with the most need are least aware of programs.

(2) Those who use programs the most include those 75 to 84 years old, those with a number of group memberships, those with more need, those who are most aware of programs, and those with the least education.

While those who have needs are most likely to use programs, they are also among those who have the least awareness of programs to begin with. Since awareness is an important factor leading to program utilization, this seems to filter out many who have real needs.

Looking at the findings somewhat differently, the frail elderly with the greatest needs are not being reached effectively. Since awareness of programs is one important factor leading to actual program utilization, the process of disengagement associated with greater age seems to screen out many with real needs. Key policy implications seem to follow from our analysis. First, citizens' awareness of programs' existence must be raised—especially among the oldest-old and those with greater needs. Access programs are clearly called for. For instance, area agencies on aging could sponsor outreach volunteer programs with those volunteers making contact with the oldest-old to inform them of programs which might help them. Telephone canvassing with appropriate followup for those with needs might be one useful tactic. If additional funding were forthcoming, special outreach programs could be devised to more directly tie those with needs to programs capable of meeting needs. Needs assessment surveys could be sponsored to enhance the precision of targeting. We discuss a series of tactics designed to enhance outreach in Chapter 7.

In addition, we found that those involved in groups are more aware of programs and use them more frequently. This suggests that efforts to get more of the "at-risk" population involved in groups might be useful. Groups provide information and support for their members; this, in turn, translates into more program awareness and greater actual use of programs. It is, of course, not possible to get all of those persons with needs involved in groups—many choose not to associate extensively with others. Nonetheless, working to increase group involvement could be another way of enhancing program use by those with greater needs.

This set of tactics could produce a better correspondence between the oldest-old and programs to meet their needs. As we have seen, the oldest-old have the most needs, the least group involvement, the lowest sense of control over their lives, the least education. Consequently, they are also least aware of programs and use programs the least. Since one of the groups specified for targeting by area agencies on aging is the oldest-old, our suggestions are aimed at an important issue. While our findings are limited to one rural county, and we know that rural elderly have different needs from those in more urban areas (Kim, 1983), they may apply in urban areas as well. To answer this question and to provide additional suggestions on better linking those with needs to programs designed to help them, more comparative research is required.

Older Females

Previous literature on program encounters in both gerontology and political science lumps males and females together. Chapter 4 presents several categories of predictive variables, among which are: personal resources; social resources; need; program-related factors; values and beliefs.

This model identifies key variables that ought to predict program awareness (as intervening variable) as well as program use. Literature tells us that females have greater need and fewer resources than older males. Thus, different dynamics ought to shape program encounters for females as opposed to males. Data analysis below examines patterns of findings separately for older men and women to gain a clearer picture of gender differences and the peculiar challenges facing older females.

Once more, we rely on the 1983 survey of Allegany County older Americans. Among this group, 30% live in rural areas (on farms or in the country); the mean age is 74.6 years old (57% are young-old, 31% are 75 to 84; 12% are oldest-old). The average education level is somewhat less than receipt of a high school diploma. Mean family income for older women is about $7500 (although the median is only $5500 and the mode $4500). Overall, females live longer, are poorer, and less educated than their male counterparts in Allegany County.

The central dependent variables are program awareness and program use. The independent variables are those identified in the model for predicting program use that we constructed in Chapter 4: social resources (for later analysis, we also created a summed index of social resources; this overall index is arrived at in the following manner: each person was given one point for each of the following responses—living in a village as opposed to out in the countryside, being young-old [74 and younger], being married, having a number of group memberships, expressing the existence of a support network, having completed education beyond high school, being able to get around, and participating in partisan activities); personal resources (An overall index of personal resources was constructed in a manner analogous to the social resources index above; people were awarded one point for each of the following—expressing very high levels of life satisfaction, expressing an interest in politics, feeling politically efficacious, and indicating strong internal locus of control); need; a surrogate measure of program characteristics is program awareness; "values and beliefs" is represented by the indicator described in Chapter 4.

Findings. There is variation in the two program variables. Program awareness among females has a mean of 16.1, a median and mode of 16. The standard deviation is 6.3. Each female respondent uses a mean of 2.1 programs (the median is 2 and the mode is 1), with a standard deviation of 1.9. By comparison, older males are aware of a mean of 16.3 programs (not statistically different from females' awareness level) and use a mean of 1.5 programs (a very statistically significant difference). It is relevant to note that males have more social and personal resources than females and far fewer needs (t-tests yield significant differences in all these cases). The latter is consistent with the more general literature noted in the introduction to this chapter.

Table 5.4 reports the Pearson's correlation coefficients among the variables discussed above—for both males and females.

Those females who are more aware of programs have less need, greater political interest and efficacy and sense of mastery over their lives. They also have more group ties, greater education levels, and more partisan activity. Additionally, they are less old, married, and

Table 5.4. Multiple Regression Analysis: Predicting Program Awareness.

	Females (N = 284)		Males (N = 132)	
	r	*Beta*	*r*	*Beta*
Personal Resources				
Political interest	.30**	.13**	.20**	.04
Political efficacy	.16**	−.01	.20**	−.03
Internal locus of control	.20**	.03	.21**	.06
Life satisfaction	.02	.08	−.13**	.06
Social Resources				
Rural	−.06	−.08	−.06	.03
Group membership	.36**	.29**	.42**	.42**
Social support	.05	−.11**	.09	−.11
Age	−.32**	−.29**	−.35**	−.23**
Education	.43**	.29**	.32**	.13
Party-oriented activities	.26**	−.02	.22**	−.08
Married	.10*	.01	.29**	.11
Mobility	.12**	−.02	.25**	.10
Need	−.20**	−.09	−.21**	.08
Individualistic Values	−.01	−.05	.02	.00
Multiple R		.61		.56
Multiple R²		.37		.32
Significance		.0000		.0000

* P < .10
**P < .05

mobile (facing no transportation difficulties). The women who are most familiar with programs, then, have ample personal and social resources and, ironically, less need for programs' services.

Those with the greatest needs and fewest resources are least cognizant of programs. For males, the same basic pattern emerges. The one difference is that greater life satisfaction becomes associated with less program awareness. For neither males nor females are individualistic values related to program awareness.

Of course, zero-order relationships may prove misleading. Listwise multiple regression analysis was undertaken to determine the impact of each independent variable while allowing them to "compete" with all others (see Table 5.4). Among females, political interest is the only personal resource to retain any relationship with program awareness. The social resources with an impact on awareness include more group memberships and greater education, along with less social support and lower age. Need's impact largely disappears. The explained variation is a robust .37 (with a multiple correlation of .61).

For males, as Table 5.4 shows, no personal resources remain linked with awareness. The only two social resources to have any impact are more group memberships and lower age. Need essentially drops out (and, oddly enough, changes signs). 32% of the variation is explained with a multiple R of .56.

What of actual use of programs? Table 5.5 demonstrates that, for females, use goes up with greater need, as one would expect. Personal resources have a mixed set of relationships: interest in politics is linked with more use; political efficacy and internal locus of control are correlated with less program usage. Social resources such as group membership and social support vary directly with actual use. On the other hand, being married depresses use. Program awareness elevates program use. Individualistic values are unrelated to program use.

With males, personal resources are unrelated to program usage (see Table 5.5). Rurality decreases use of programs, while group memberships and social support boost it. Greater need and program awareness are also linked, at the zero-level, with utilization. Values are unrelated to the dependent variable.

Once more, multivariate analysis is in order, to see what the relative contribution of each predictor variable is while taking into account the effects of all the others. Table 5.5 reports the standardized regression coefficients (betas) from listwise multiple regression.

Actual use of programs by females is most influenced by group memberships; more need and program awareness also serve as predictors of greater program use. Being married and receiving more education depress levels of usage. Explained variation is a modest 20%. For males, the weightiest predictors (in order of descending impact) are: group memberships, program awareness, and education (an inverse relationship). 19% of the variation is explained, with a multiple R of .44—respectable but not outstanding.

To get a greater sense of the dynamics underlying program use, path analysis was conducted. For the path analysis, the predictor variables used include need, program awareness, individualistic values, and the

Table 5.5. Multiple Regression Anaysis: Predicting Program Use.

	Females (N = 284)		Males (N = 132)	
	r	Beta	r	Beta
Personal Resources				
Political interest	.10*	.09	.00	.01
Political efficacy	−.09*	−.06	−.08	−.08
Internal locus of control	−.09*	−.03	−.05	−.05
Life satisfaction	.00	.09	−.05	.06
Social Resources				
Rural	−.06	−.03	−.11*	−.10
Group membershp	.28**	.31**	.28**	.38**
Social support	.17**	−.06	.15**	−.13
Age	.03	.02	.11	.12
Education	−.02	−.14**	−.10	−.17*
Party-oriented activity	.04	.03	.03	.06
Married	−.22**	−.20**	−.08	−.13
Mobility	−.06	.08	'ms.01	−.01
Need	.18**	.27**	.14*	.12
Individualistic Values	.05	.06	−.04	−.02
Program Awareness	.12**	.12*	.19**	.20**
Multiple R		.45		.44
Multiple R²		.20		.19
Significance		.0000		.0000

* P < .10
**P < .05

indices of social resources and personal resources. Table 5.6 summarizes the network of correlations among these variables and program use. The pattern for males and females seems quite similar here, with program awareness and need level as key shapers of program use. For both sexes, greater personal and social resources and lower need predict to greater program awareness. Individualistic values are only very mildly associated with the other variables.

Table 5.6.   Pearson's r: Correlation Matrices, By Gender.

Females (N = 301)

	Program awareness	Program use	Personal resources	Social resources	Need	Values
Program awareness	—	.16**	.19**	.40**	−.19**	−.01
Program use		—	−.03	.03	.18**	.03
Personal resources			—	.39**	−.40**	.09*
Social resources				—	−.28**	.01
Need					—	−.12**
Individualistic values						—

Males (N = 140)

	Program awareness	Program use	Personal resources	Social resources	Need	Values
Program awareness	—	.20**	.34**	.40**	−.23**	−.01
Program use		—	−.10	.06	.13*	−.05
Personal resources			—	.32**	−.50**	.10
Social resources				—	−.35**	−.02
Need					—	
Individualistic values						—

* P < .10
**P < .05

Figure 5.1 reports two regression-based path analyses. The path coefficients represent standardized regression coefficients (betas significant at .05 or less) from stepwise multiple regression analysis. It becomes apparent that the dynamics by which people come to use programs differ by gender. For older women, personal resources are not a part of the web of relationships at all. Greater social resources seem to reduce need level and increase program awareness. In turn,

Figure 5.1. Path Models: Predicting Program Use, by Gender.

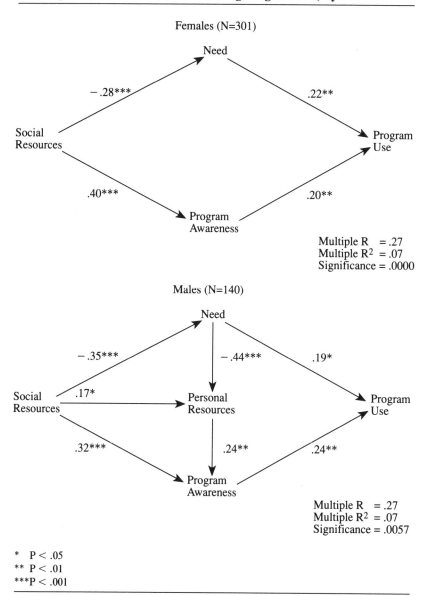

Females (N=301)

Multiple R   = .27
Multiple R^2 = .07
Significance = .0000

Males (N=140)

Multiple R   = .27
Multiple R^2 = .07
Significance = .0057

*   P < .05
** P < .01
***P < .001

greater need and awareness increase the number of programs actually used. The 7% explained variation is quite modest, and may indicate that using the summed indices reduces explanatory power (compare with Table 5.3 and the 20% explained variation).

For males, a different pattern emerges. Personal resources come into play, being grafted, as it were, onto the female pattern. Greater need is tied to fewer personal resources, as more abundant social resources enhance level of personal resources. In their turn, personal resources are linked to greater program awareness. Explained variation remains at a small 7%. In terms of work on gender differences, as discussed below, this distinction makes sense.

Discussion. First, to summarize basic findings:

(1) Zero-order correlations show that personal resources are tied to greater program awareness and have a mixed effect on program use; social resources have a rather mixed set of relationships with use but consistently are tied to greater awareness; need is associated with less awareness but with more actual program use; program awareness is correlated with both greater use. The same pattern obtains for both older men and older women.

(2) Listwise multiple regression indicates that greater social resources are the most important predictors of elevated awareness; more need and greater program awareness shape increased program use, while social resources have a mixed impact. Personal resources largely drop out as predictors of both need and awareness. Again, the patterns are congruent for older men and women.

(3) Path analysis reveals that personal resources come to have an indirect impact on program use among older males, whereas these factors are not at all part of the model predicting program use for older females. Explained variation in both cases is quite modest.

What do these findings tell us? First, older females and males with greater needs are not likely to know about programs' existence any more than those without any major needs. If one believes that programs ought to be made more accessible to those with needs, outreach programs to better inform older females (and males) facing problems seem advisable. This is especially so since program awareness is one factor influencing the actual use of programs' services. Given⁺ that older women have many more problems than older males, this finding is particularly significant. Simply, greater efforts must be undertaken to link needy older women (and their male counterparts) to programs designed to meet those needs.

Second, while predictors used in this paper do a reasonable job of explaining people's level of awareness, they are not as effective in telling one why older women (and men) use programs. Perhaps the addition of better value and ideological variables would lead to enhanced explanation. A modest but reasonable level of explained variation of program use is characteristic of other research; such findings may be saying that new approaches or better measures are needed. Perhaps a more determined effort to measure stigmatization of individuals for using means-tested programs, as Nelson (1980) suggests, could assist. At any rate, more work clearly needs to be done to explain this facet of older women's' public lives.

Third, one specific finding from Table 5.6 warrants a comment. There, one can see that females who are married use more programs than unmarried older women; being an older male who is married has no impact on program use as compared with unmarried older male status. This may reflect a peculiar family dynamic. Females are more likely, one might hypothesize, to pay attention to their spouses when using programs is discussed, whereas older males may not pay any particular attention to what their wives have to say. This would represent a more traditional view that women are less competent in the larger public sphere.

The final point to be addressed is why the patterns in path analysis differ between older men and older women. Recall that personal resources turn out to have an indirect influence on program use through their effects on program awareness among older men. There is no such impact of personal resources with older women. This may be a function of women, generally, being more socially oriented than men; men tend to be more likely to draw upon personal resources and not be as tied to social networks. Older males, for instance, tend to be less intimate in their friendships and social ties than older women. This would seem to allow more ''play'' for an impact of personal factors on males (e.g., Andersen, 1988). This may imply that different approaches are in order to try to reach older women versus older men. Needy older males, more likely to draw upon their personal resources, may be harder to reach than older women.

However, the results of the path analysis do not lend themselves to easy interpretation, and to go much further at this point is to risk going well beyond what the data will bear. The comments in the preceding paragraph can only be taken as suggestive. Further work might well focus upon differences between males and females in terms of personal as opposed to social resources. If the suggestions raised in this paper are correct, such corroborating evidence could be useful in delineating distinct strategies of outreach for older males as against older females.

It seems clear that some policy implications must be addressed. Outreach programs at the state and national level have suffered budget cuts in recent years. But the findings of this paper clearly imply that older females with the greatest needs are simply not very well aware of programs designed to meet those needs. The most obvious approach to addressing this gap between need and use is to re-emphasize outreach.

Rurality

Public officials need to be aware of the interaction between rural elderly and their environments. Much of the existing literature on goodness of fit between elderly and their environments (e.g., see Kahana, 1975; Lawton, 1977) has focused on the effects of that fit on sense of personal well-being. And there has been little work exploring the effects of the rural-less rural dimension. Lawton et al. (1980) found public policy implications of the goodness of fit position; although environments generally had only a small independent impact on well-being, the authors concluded that environmentally based interventions could enhance well-being more practically than intervention strategies based on trying to change the individual. One project has explicitly examined rurality's relationship to well-being. Windley and Scheidt (1980) utilized a rural breakdown into three categories—0 to 500 person towns, 501 to 1500 population areas, and 1501 to 2500 person communities—to predict well-being of the elderly. Indeed, rurality had an impact—albeit small. However, to this point there has really been no study that has applied this "goodness of fit" approach to explaining program use and other elements of the rural elderly's public lives.

A number of expectations follow from a full elaboration of the goodness of fit model:

1. People living in villages (as opposed to living in the country) have greater access to social services due to their proximity to service delivery agencies. Thus, one would predict that program aware-

ness and use would be higher within villages than out in the country.

2. More rural areas are reputed to be disadvantaged with respect to education, health, housing, and transportation when compared to their more urban counterparts; therefore, there should be greater strain and discomfort associated with living outside of villages.

3. Verba and Nie (1972) have pointed out that one model of explaining level of politicization is the "mobilization model," i.e., as people move from more isolated to less isolated areas, they should become more politicized because of the greater extent of social networks, the greater social interaction, and so on. Hence, we would expect that those who live in the country will be less politicized (that is, less active in and informed about politics).

The 358 respondents from the 1987 Allegany County survey represent the data base for this part of the chapter. We use the 1987 data because these contain measures of psychological well-being as well as psychological function. Subjects were classified as residing in a rural ecology if they lived on a farm or outside a village boundary. Subjects living within a village were classified as "less rural." In all, 119 persons live in rural areas (33%) while 238 (67%) reside in less rural areas (i.e., in villages).

The dependent variables include program use (the measure used in 1987 has a somewhat different set of programs than the 1983 survey; however, the construction of the overall index is the same), program awareness, political efficacy, political interest, trust in government, locus of control, personality (neuroticism, openness, and extroversion—based on Costa and McCrae's instrument), extent to which the person held personal and social resources. Control variables include age, sex, education. We also included a set of variables assessing the state of each person's life, such as health status, nutritional level, extent to which respondents had deficits in activities of daily living, and type and extent of problems faced.

Findings. Table 5.7 summarizes the characteristics of those who live in rural versus less rural areas. The pattern of Pearson's correlations is not terribly strong, but a pattern there is. Those living in the more rural parts of this rural county are more apt to be male, less educated, less needy, homeowners, possessed of fewer social resources upon which to draw, less churchgoing. They also have fewer transportation problems and are longer-term residents.

Table 5.8 explores the effects of rurality on the key dependent

Table 5.7. Demographic Correlates of Rurality, N = 358.

	Rural
Group membership	−.04
Need level	−.11**
Male	.08*
Age	−.07*
Education	−.09**
Number of unmet needs	−.05
Deficits in activities of daily living	−.07
Homeowner	.11**
Regularity of church attendance	−.07*
Transportation problems	−.10**
Social support network	.06
Personal resources	.00
Social resources	−.21****
Problems paying bills	.02
Length of residence in area	.09**

```
*    P < .10
**   P < .05
***  P < .01
****P < .001
```

variables. Here, we see rather few strong effects. The Pearson's correlation coefficients suggest that greater rurality goes with less program use, somewhat lower political efficacy, more cynicism about government, greater Republican partisanship, and less openness. Given previous research findings suggesting an impact on well-being, it is interesting to note that life satisfaction, an index of subjective well-being, is unrelated to rurality.

Table 5.8 also reports partial correlation coefficients, controlling for sex, age, and education. In the main, the pattern revealed by the zero-order correlations holds up, although the magnitude of the partial coefficients remains very slight. Generally, the results suggest that those living in the most rural parts of the county use programs less, are somewhat less politicized, and are rather closed minded (also defined as "down to earth, practical, traditional, and pretty much set in their ways"). There is no relationship to life satisfaction, one global indicator of well-being.

Discussion. In one sense, given the paucity of robust findings, it might be appropriate to simply say that rurality is not a significant

**Table 5.8. Partial Correlations: Predicting Aspects of Respondents'
Public Lives, Controlling Sex, Age, and Education, N = 342.**

	Rural	
	r	*Beta*
Trust in government	− .09**	− .08*
Conservative ideology	− .02	− .02
Approval of Ronald Reagan	− .02	.00
Republican partisanship	.08*	.09*
Neurotic personality	− .06	− .07
Extroversion	− .01	− .02
Openness	− .12**	− .12***
Internal locus of control	.04	.04
Political participation index	− .03	− .03
Life satisfaction	.06	.06
Program awareness	− .01	− .01
Program use	− .10**	− .10**
Political efficacy	− .08*	− .08*
Political interest	− .04	− .04

*   P < .10
**   P < .05
***   P < .01
****P < .001

ecological predictor of people's well-being and their public lives.
However, that may be too strong a conclusion. There is, after all, a
very modest pattern that makes some sense emerging from the data.
Those living in more rural areas tend to use programs less—partly we
suspect because programs are less accessible and largely because those
living in more rural areas tend to be in good shape, have reasonable
transportation, and so on. The data are consistent with the view that
those living in rural areas whose health begins to fail will move to the
villages or larger population areas in order to get services needed. The
people in the countryside seem less politically attuned (they are less
efficacious and less trusting of government). Overall, their public lives
bear a lower profile than their peers living in villages.

References

Andersen, Margaret L. 1988. *Thinking About Women*. New York: MacMillan,
    2nd edition.

Andersen, Ronald and John F. Newman. 1973. Societal and individual determinants of medical care utilization in the United States. *Milbank Memorial
Fund Quarterly* 51: 95–124.

Block, Marilyn R., Janice L. Davidson, and Jean D. Grambs. 1981. *Women
over Forty*. New York: Springer Publishing Company.

Brown, Steven D. 1982. The explanation of particularized contacting. *Urban
Affairs Quarterly* 18: 217–234.

Butler, R. N. 1980. *The Older Women: Continuities and Discontinuities*.
Washington, D. C.: Department of Health and Human Services.

Feller, B. A. 1983. *Americans Need Help to Function at Home*. Hyattsville:
National Center for Health Statistics.

Fowles, D. 1983. The changing older population. *Aging* May-June: 6–11.

Kahana, E. 1975. A congruence model of person-environment interaction. In
F. D. Byerts, M. Powell Lawton, and J. Newcumber (eds.), *Theory Devel-
opment in Environments and Aging*. Washington, D. C.: Gerontological
Society of America.

Katz, Daniel, Barbara A. Gutek, Robert C. Kahn, and Eugenia Barton. 1975.
Bureaucratic Encounters. Ann Arbor: Institute for Social Research.

Kim, Paul K. H. 1983. Public Policies for the Rural Elderly. In William P.
Browne and Laura Katz Olson (eds.), *Aging and Public Policy*. Westport,
CT: Greenwood Press.

Krout, John A. 1983a. Correlates of service utilization among the rural elderly.
The Gerontologist 23: 500–504.

Krout, John A. 1983b. Knowledge and use of services by the elderly. *International Journal of Aging and Human Development* 17: 153–167.

Krout, John A. 1986. *The Aged in Rural America*. Westport, CT: Greenwood
Press.

Lammers, William W. 1983. *Public Policy and the Aging*. Washington, D. C.:
CQ Press.

Lawton, M. Powell. 1977. The impact of the environment on aging and
behavior. In J. E. Birren and K. W. Schaie (eds), *Handbook of the Psychology of Aging*. New York: Van Nostrand.

Lawton, M. Powell, L. Nehemow, and T. M. Yeh. 1980. Neighborhood
environment and the well-being of older tenants in planned housing. *International Journal of Aging and Human Development* 2: 211–227.

Lowy, Lewis. 1985. *Social Work with the Aging*. New York: Longman (2nd
edition).

Maiden, Robert, Thomas A. Leitko, and Steven A. Peterson. 1984. Rural
elderly. Presented at Gerontological Society of America, San Antonio,
Texas.

Minkler, Meredith and Robyn Stone. 1985. The feminization of poverty and
older women. *The Gerontologist* 25: 351–357.

Moen, Elizabeth. 1978. The reluctance of the elderly to accept services. *Social
Problems* 25: 293–303.

Moon, M. and I. V. Sawhill. 1983. Family incomes: gainers and losers. In J. C. Palmer and Isabel V. Sawhill (eds.), *The Reagan Record*. Cambridge: Ballinger.

Nelson, Barbara J. 1980. Help-seeking from public authorities. *Policy Sciences* 12: 175–192.

Nelson, Barbara J. 1984. Women's poverty and women's citizenship. *Signs* 10: 209–230.

New York State Office for the Aging (1986). *Orientation Primer for New York State Area Agency Advisory Councils*.

Peterson, Steven A. 1986. Close encounters of the bureaucratic kind. *American Journal of Political Science* 30: 347–356.

Peterson, Steven A. 1987. Older citizens' program encounters. *Journal of Applied Gerontology* 6: 39–52.

Peterson, Steven A. 1988. Stay tuned to your programs: explaining older Americans' program encounters. *Journal of Aging Studies* 2: 183–197.

Preston, S. 1984a. Children and the elderly: divergent paths for America's dependents. *Demography* 21: 44–49.

Preston, S. 1984b. Children and the elderly in the United States. *Scientific American* 251: 44–49.

Rosenwaike, I. 1985. *The Extreme Aged in America*. Westport, CT: Greenwood Press.

Sharp, Elaine B. 1982. Citizen-initiated contacting of government officials and socioeconomic status. *American Political Science Review* 76: 109–115.

Snider, Earle L. 1980. Factors influencing health service knowledge among the elderly. *Journal of Health and Social Behavior* 21: 371–377.

Suzman, R. and Matilda White Riley. 1985. Introducing the 'oldest-old.' *Milbank Memorial Fund Quarterly* 63: 177–186.

Thomas, John Clayton 1982. Citizen-initiated contacts with government agencies. *American Journal of Political Science* 26: 504–522.

Verba, Sidney and Norman H. Nie. 1972. *Participation in America*. New York: Harper & Row.

Ward, Russell A. 1977. Services for older people. *Journal of Health and Social Behavior* 18: 61–70.

Ward, Russell A., Susan R. Sherman, and Mark LaGory. 1984. Informal networks and knowledge of services for older persons. *Journal of Gerontology* 39: 216–223.

Warlick, Jennifer L. 1983. Aged women in poverty: a problem without a solution? In William P. Browne and Laura Katz Olson (eds.), *Aging and Public Policy*. Westport, CT: Greenwood Press.

Windley, P. G. and R. J. Scheidt. 1980. The well-being of older persons in small rural towns. *Educational Gerontology* 355–373.

Zuckerman, Alan S. and Darrell M. West. 1985. The political bases of citizen contacting. *American Political Science Review* 79: 117–131.

Chapter 6
Case Studies: Issue Areas

Introduction

We have discussed the extent to which our sample of rural older Americans is aware of and uses programs designed to meet their needs. To this point, though, our discussion has been at the aggregate level—not at the level of specific policy areas, such as nutrition, social needs, housing, and mental health. In this chapter, we explore each of these areas. We examine what factors are associated with problems actually occurring and how people come (or do not come) to use programs. For each policy area, we discuss implications for decision-makers as these emerge.

Nutrition Policy

The first part of this chapter explores the extent of nutritional problems and the use of programs designed to address these problems by a sample of rural elderly. We use the 1987 Allegany County data to explore the applicability of the model outlined in chapter 4 designed to predict who uses programs to the area of nutrition.

Research on the nutritional needs of the elderly is not as extensive as one might think. Interest in nutrition is a rather recent phenomenon, emerging as a result of sociodemographic factors and health status of the elderly in the context of overall government programs for this group (Smicklas-Wright and Fosmire, 1985).

Awareness of the elderly's nutritional needs first began to be noticed in detail in the late 1960s. Senator George McGovern declared (National Council on the Aging, 1971: 28): "[They] form the most uni-

111

formly malnourished segment of our population" (See U. S. Senate, Part 14, *Nutrition and the Aged*, 1971). Later studies continued to find major nutritional problems facing mature Americans (Kovar, 1977; Kohrs, O'Hanlon, and Eklund, 1978; Rawson *et al.*, 1978; Ryan, Craig, and Finn, 1992). Any number of factors affect nutritional status of the elderly—from general health status to dental problems to declining sensory acuity to the use of certain prescription drugs to depression to low income (e.g., Chernoff and Lipschitz, 1988; Chernoff, 1987; Smicklas-Wright and Fosmire, 1985).

Two major nutritional programs designed explicitly for older Americans are congregate meals and mobile meals. The first provides group meals at community centers so that those who can travel can enjoy their meals in the company of others. The elderly who need meals but are unable to travel to the sites can have meals delivered to their homes (mobile meals). People aged 60 and above are eligible for these two programs. A third program that the elderly also have access to is Food Stamps. This is a voucher-type plan where individuals who are eligible (this is a means-tested program) receive vouchers from the government redeemable by grocers and others.

To this point, there has been rather little evaluation of the effects of these nutrition programs. Suggestive findings, though, indicate that participation ameliorates some important nutritional problems (e.g., Weiner, 1982; Kohrs *et al.*, 1980) and may have social and economic benefits for individuals as well (Smicklas-Wright and Fosmire, 1985), although there is considerable debate over the findings (e.g., Posner, 1979; Estes and Freeman, 1976).

Data suggest that those with the greatest nutritional difficulties include those living alone, with limited mobility, and experiencing a variety of health problems (Frongillo *et al.*, 1987). Ironically, those most likely to be reached by nutritional programs tend to be more socially active, involved with their communities, and participant in more out-of-home activities (Hassen *et al.*, 1978), thus leaving many elderly unreached by these programs. In New York, for instance, Cahill (1984) reports that only 12% of the elderly take part in nutrition programs, whereas the need is estimated to be considerably higher than that. In this section, we use multivariate analysis to identify the array of variables that best predicts program awareness and utilization.

Previous literature on program encounters in both gerontology and political science suggests several categories of predictive variables (See chapter 4). In this section, we apply the formulation designed to integrate the political science and gerontology literatures that appears in Chapter 4 to the area of nutrition. Key independent variables are (1) Personal resources, (2) Social resources, (3) Need, (4) Program-related factors, (5) Values and beliefs. We use the 1987 data base in this analysis because of its superior coverage of nutrition programs (the 1983 questionnaire, for instance, did not inquire about awareness of and use of Food Stamps in the same format as the rest of the nutrition programs).

An additional word is in order about our measure of values in the 1987 questionnaire. The standard argument is that rugged individualists are less likely to use programs. Hence, explicit measures of individualist views are included in this study. One is self-identified conservative ideology. Conservatives are more likely to extol the individual who makes it on his or her own or to criticize the person who "sups at the public trough." In addition, a three item index (coming from Feldman, 1982) was constructed to get at an individualistic orientation. Agreement with the statements that "Poor people don't have the ability to get ahead" and that "Some people who don't get ahead in life blame the system when they really have only themselves to blame" and disagreement that "Competition . . . is often wasteful and destructive" gives each person a score of from 0 to 3 on the individualism scale.

Dependent variables include awareness of three nutrition programs offered within the county (Office for the Aging Mobile Meals and Congregate Dining, Food Stamps) and extent to which these three programs are used. Each respondent was asked how many out of these three programs they were aware of and how many they have actually used.

Need is a summed index indicating the extent of nutritional problems faced by the individual. Three items comprise this index: reporting eating only one meal per day, saying that one does not have a good diet, and indicating that there is a problem in eating regularly or getting enough to eat. Eighty-five per cent of the people report no nutritional difficulties; however, the other 15% claim to have some problem with diet or eating.

Findings. First, there is variation in the two dependent variables. Program awareness is high, but a modest minority of respondents— 14% of the total—are not familiar with all three programs. Clearly, the vast majority, though, are well aware of these programs (lack of awareness is a significant problem in other program areas that have been studied). Most respondents use none of these programs, although 1 out of 3 has used at least one. Table 6.1 indicates the extent of awareness of and use of each of the three programs.

Table 6.1. Frequencies: Nutrition Program Encounters, N = 358.

	Aware of		Use		Satisfied	
	N	%	N	%	N	%
Congregate dining	331	93	92	26	83	90
Mobile meals	328	92	27	8	23	85
Food Stamps	336	94	36	10	31	86

Who are the people with greatest nutritional problems? A simple correlational analysis in Table 6.2 answers this question. In short, having nutritional problems goes with less of a sense of mastery over one's life, neuroticism, physical infirmities, fewer group memberships, being female, greater age, less education, being unmarried, not being mobile, and coming from the village of Wellsville (the largest village in the county).

Table 6.3 reports the Pearson's correlation coefficients between the independent variables and each of the dependent variables.

Those who are more aware of the programs have less need, more personal resources (greater political interest, life satisfaction, efficacy, internal locus of control and fewer physical infirmities and mental problems), greater social resources (married, more educated, being politically participant, having group memberships, being mobile, not coming from the northern part of the county [the most isolated segment of Allegany County], being younger). Individualistic values are associated with greater awareness. People who are most familiar with programs, then, have ample personal and social resources and, ironically, somewhat less need for programs' services. Those with the greatest needs and fewest resources are least cognizant of programs. This suggests a real mismatch of need and awareness.

Actual use of programs, however, does go with greater need. Having ample personal resources generally is inversely related to program use: interest in politics is linked with less use, as are life satisfaction and internal locus of control. Physical infirmity, representing a serious drain on one's personal resources, is tied to greater program use, as is neuroticism. Social resources such as coming from the northern part of the county, being married, having mobility, and being male are inversely associated with use. On the other hand, being older enhances extent of program use. Greater need goes with greater use, as one should expect. Program awareness, surprisingly, is not related to program use. The low level of variation for program awareness may

Table 6.2. Pearson's r: Correlates of Self-Reported Nutritional
Problems (N = 345).

	Poor nutrition
Internal locus of control	−.23****
Neuroticism	.20****
Physical infirmities	.12**
Group memberships	−.23****
Male	−.12**
Age	.10**
Education level	−.07*
Married	−.12**
Mobility	−.23****
Northern part of county	−.01
Wellsville residence	.10**

*   P < .10
**   P < .05
***   P < .01
****P < .001

attenuate what one would expect to be a robust correlation. Finally, values. While conservatism is unrelated, individualistic values are correlated with program use. In the end, having personal and social resources are associated with lower program use, whereas individualistic values and need are tied to greater use. Individualism, of course, is related in a manner *contrary* to our expectations. We have no ready explanation for this—other than that it might be due to interaction with other independent variables.

Multivariate analysis is in order, to see what the relative contribution of each predictor variable is while taking into account the effects of all the others. Table 6.4 reports the standardized regression coefficients (betas) from listwise multiple regression.

The weightiest predictors of program awareness—in order—are political interest (inversely), internal locus of control, coming from the northern part of the county (inversely), having mobility, and being male (inversely). In total, the independent variables explain about 16% of the variation in program awareness. Note also that need completely drops out when personal and social resources are controlled. Thus, personal resources and social resources are all that are left to predict awareness.

Actual use of programs is most influenced by more group member-

Table 6.3. Pearson's r: Predictors of Nutritional Program Awareness and Use, N = 321.

	Nutrition Program Awareness	Nutrition Program Use
Personal Resources		
Political interest	−.02	−.18****
Political efficacy	.13***	−.05
Internal locus of control	.26****	−.12**
Life satisfaction	.14***	−.11**
Mental health problems	−.19****	.18**
Physical infirmities	−.09*	.18****
Social Resources		
Northern part of county	−.16***	−.11****
Group membership	.14***	.04
Age	−.09*	.13***
Education	.16***	−.02
Political participation	.12**	−.04
Married	.11**	−.14***
Mobility	.22****	−.20****
Church attendance	.07	−.01
Male	−.02	−.19****
Need (Nutritional problems)	−.07*	.16***
Program Awareness	—	.06
Values		
Individualistic values	.08*	.09*
Conservative identification	−.02	.00

*   P < .10
** P < .05
*** P < .01
****P < .001

ships, more program awareness, being female, having mobility problems, not being politically interested, and having mental health problems and coming from the southern part of Allegany County. Explained variation is a modest 18%. Most interestingly, need drops out as a predictor of nutrition program usage—a finding that some

Table 6.4. Standardized Regression Coefficients (Listwise): Predictors with Nutritional Program Awareness and Use, N = 321.

	Nutrition Program Awareness	Nutrition Program Use
Personal Resources		
Political interest	− .19***	− .15**
Political efficacy	.07	.06
Internal locus of control	.17***	− .04
Life satisfaction	.04	.00
Mental health problems	− .06	.13**
Physical infirmities	.01	.08
Social Resources		
Northern part of county	− .13**	− .12**
Group membership	.05	.27***
Age	− .05	.03
Education	.05	− .03
Political participation	.08	.07
Married	.05	− .03
Mobility	.13**	− .13**
Church attendance	− .06	− .10
Male	− .12*	− .15**
Need (Nutritional problems)	.00	.08
Program Awareness	—	.07*
Values		
Individualistic values	.07	.08
Conservative identification	− .03	.02
Multiple R	.40	.42
Multiple R^2	.16	.18
Significance	.0000	.0000

*   P < .10
**   P < .05
*** P < .01
****P < .001

might interpret as suggesting a need-service gap. However, as already pointed out, actual use seems fairly widespread.

Discussion. First, to summarize basic findings:

(1) Programs to help the elderly with nutritional problems are well known and reasonably heavily used.

(2) Zero-order correlations show that personal resources are tied to greater program awareness and less program use; just so, social resources tend to go with greater awareness and less use; need is associated with less awareness but with more actual program use; program awareness is correlated with use.

(3) Listwise multiple regression indicates that greater social and personal resources are the most important predictors of elevated awareness; fewer social and personal resources go with greater use (although rather few of these have any real effect). Greater program awareness shapes increased program use.

What do these findings tell us? First, older Americans from this rural sample with greater needs are not likely to know about programs' existence any more than those without any major needs. If one believes that programs ought to be made more accessible to those with needs, outreach programs to better inform eligible recipients of services facing problems seem advisable. This is especially so since program awareness is one factor influencing the actual use of programs' services. Of course, program awareness is already so high that this would doubtless have only the most marginal of effects on reducing any need-use gap.

Some evidence, though, independent from our study, suggests one possible problem—confusion about eligibility and the marketing of the programs and outreach efforts (Posner, 1979). Many citizens who seek out information about eligibility for such programs are stymied by government actions. For instance, a report by the New York City Comptroller notes that (1988: 1):

> People who need Food Stamps often have great difficulty reaching dispensing centers by phone and are almost always given incomplete or wrong information, even when they do get through, an investigation by Comptroller Goldin has disclosed. In just 4.2% of all calls made in the investigation were callers given correct and complete information.

And this is probably just as true in rural areas. It might well be that an effort to provide better information to those who inquire about nutritional programs could be useful. Regrettably, our data cannot speak to the issue of whether or not referral mechanisms have any effects on program awareness and use. However, this is likely to be so and calls for further exploration.

Second, in future research, it may be that we have to seek other predictor variables or other models of explaining variation in program awareness and use. Low levels of explained variation in program use are found in many other studies; such relatively weak findings may be saying that we need new approaches or better measures. In the end, these findings may be telling us that we have to better reach out to those with social needs to link them to the appropriate programs. Since these people are outside of existing social networks, though, this will be a difficult goal to achieve.

Extensive promotional campaigns have sometimes been useful in increasing program use among rural elderly (Bender and Hart, 1987). Intensive "casefinding," having volunteers go out into the community and actively seek out the elderly with needs to link them to appropriate programs, might be another mechanism to ensure a better match between need and program (Young, Goughler, and Larson, 1986).

There are shortcomings to this study. For one thing, the sample comes from one rural county in upstate New York. Hence, external validity is an obvious problem. For another, we discuss the process of what shapes awareness of and use of nutritional programs—but our data are not longitudinal. Truly to test our expectations, we need panel data. To assess process, this is absolutely critical, as the focus on the nutritional needs of the elderly is not likely to decline in the near future given the demographic trends. Indeed, we would urge scholars in political gerontology to take this need seriously and to implement more panel studies.

Our data suggest that multiple factors are involved in program use and that the overall pattern of nutritional program use is consistent with use of more general programming available to the elderly (Krout et al., 1990; Peterson, 1988). Moreover, our data clearly show the importance of social activity in the awareness and use of nutritional programs, although the specific processes by which these factors affect dietary behavior are not revealed.

Social Life of the Elderly and Social Programs

One of the problems afflicting many older Americans is an inadequate social life, loneliness, and social isolation. In this section, we once more use the 1987 data to examine the extent to which there are social needs, respondents' awareness of programs designed to address these needs, and those factors that shape people's actual use of programs in this area. Finally, we consider possible policy implications flowing from our analysis.

Recent studies examining the correlates of social support have discovered that such support serves as a protective buffer for elderly individuals. Elderly people with good support systems put off using community sponsored social service programs as long as they can until they experience a dire need for them (Revicki and Mitchell, 1991; Bear, 1990; Ward, Sherman, and LaGory, 1984; Bowling and Browne, 1991; Wenger, 1985). But the findings in the literature to this point have been inconsistent. For instance, one study looking at the role of social support and program use among the rural elderly found that both social need and isolation were inversely related to the awareness and use of senior center programs. As the level of social involvement increased in this sample, so, too, did participation in the community sponsored social programs (Krout, Cutler, and Coward, 1990).

On the other hand, another study considering entry into residential care homes found that the role of social support depends on the situation facing the individual at the time she or he enters the program (Bear, 1990). When a person lives in the community, extant social support networks inhibited the use of formal helping systems and facilitated dependence on informal sources to meet problems. Once an individual enters a residential care home, however, dense informal social support networks predict that he or she will come to depend more upon the formal system and depend less upon the informal network for help. Oddly enough, then, the socially isolated were discharged to their homes more quickly than those who had highly developed social support systems in the wings.

The ideal that social service providers wish to meet is that those with social needs will take advantage of social service programs designed to help them, while those with social support systems will not rely on social services to meet their needs, thus allowing a better match between social need and social services. However, as the studies above indicate, this is not always the reality. This section extends the effort to understand use of social programs by comparing the effects of social support on the use of community sponsored social programs.

Once more, we call upon the model outlined in Chapter 4 as the basis for examining who is aware of and who uses programs aimed at meeting social needs of Allegany County's older Americans.

First, two questions were used to assess extent of social needs: (1) "Do you have enough social contacts?" and (2) the extent to which loneliness is a problem. A summed index stands for the degree of social needs. One point was given if the person said that he or she did not have enough contacts and a second if the person claimed that loneliness was either some or a very important problem. While 68% of the people said that they had no real social needs, 27% expressed agreement with one of the two items and 5% with both. Thus, about ⅓ of the sample seem to have experienced at least some shortcomings in their social lives.

Table 6.5 shows the extent to which Allegany County's older Americans are aware of and use programs intended to meet social needs. The vast majority of people are familiar with senior citizens clubs; a clear majority know about recreational groups. Fewer are cognizant of Friendly Visitors or Telephone Reassurance, both of which have an important social component. The only one of these programs that is much used is the senior citizens' clubs. Scarcely anyone takes advantage of Friendly Visitors or Telephone Reassurance.

We constructed summed indices for both social program awareness and social program use. In terms of awareness, 11% knew about none of the programs, 20% about one, 28% about two, 16% about three, and 26% about all four—quite a range of variation indeed. In terms of actual program use, 69% stated that they had taken part in none of the programs, 23% in one of these, 7% in two, and just one person in all four.

In Table 6.6, we summarize the Pearson's correlation coefficients between the personal resources, social resources, need, program awareness, and values, on the one hand, with program awareness and use, on the other. The strongest correlates of greater social program awareness are *less* need, greater political interest, higher levels of political efficacy and internal locus of control, less neuroticism, fewer

Table 6.5. Frequencies: Social Program Encounters, N = 358.

	Aware of		Use	
	N	%	N	%
Friendly Visitors	140	39%	1	—%
Telephone Reassurance	161	45	3	1
Senior Citizens Clubs	298	83	95	27
Recreational Groups	211	59	40	11

Table 6.6. Pearson's r: Predictors with Social Program Awareness and Use, N = 320.

	Social Program Awareness	Social Program Use
Personal Resources		
Political interest	.18****	.03
Political efficacy	.19****	−.05
Internal locus of control	.31****	.07
Life satisfaction	.13***	−.01
Mental health problems	−.21****	.01
Physical infirmities	−.19****	−.01
Social Resources		
Rural	−.08*	−.08*
Group memberships	.24****	.30****
Social support	.16***	.00
Age	−.06	.01
Education	.16***	.08*
Political participation	.18***	−.05
Married	.13***	−.05
Transportation problems	−.18****	.05
Church attendance	.18****	.21****
Male	.06	.13***
Need (Social problems)	−.19****	.00
Program awareness	—	.00
Values		
Individualistic values	.09*	.08*
Conservative identification	.08*	.07

*　　P < .10
**　 P < .05
***　P < .01
****P < .001

physical infirmities, more extensive group memberships, higher level of political participation, fewer transportation problems, and more regular church attendance. Higher program usage goes with more extensive group memberships and more routine church attendance. In that sense, involvement in groups enhances the likelihood of using programs designed to help those with social problems. In an odd sense, then, it would seem that those with less need are more likely to use programs! Extensive social networks would seem to go with a person having fewer needs for affiliation with others, after all. Next, we report multivariate analysis, using a listwise multiple regression model.

Rather little variance is explained for either program awareness (19%) or program use (16%), as Table 6.7 points out. Nonetheless, a meaningful pattern of findings does emerge. In order of importance, the strongest predictors of awareness are internal locus of control, being male, being married, having individualistic values, and feeling politically efficacious. Personal factors and values seem to predominate here, as most of the social resource variables drop out of the equation. Actual use of the programs is best predicted by more group memberships and being male—period. Here, then, social resources are most important.

Discussion. The results can be fairly easily summarized:

1. Need, social and personal factors, and values all have some correlation with program awareness. Social factors, program awareness, and individualistic values are associated with program use.
2. Multiple regression analysis shows that most of the zero-order relationships disappear. A few personal and social factors and individualistic values end up still being related to program awareness. Only group membership (quite strongly) and being male remain tied to program use.

So, what does this suggest? Program awareness does not seem very much related to actual program use—so that cannot be, apparently, a very useful channel for getting the elderly with social needs into the appropriate programs. More relevant, the results suggest, would be working through existing groups within the community. The irony, of course, is that if one has a number of group memberships, one is unlikely to have great need for such programs! Indeed, we find that group memberships have a Pearson's correlation with social need of $-.23$. Thus, those who, through their group memberships, use existing programs are probably among the least needy in this area.

The challenge, then, would seem to be to try to develop a better matchup between need and program use. Note the $-.14$ beta in Table 6.7 between social needs and use of programs designed to address

Table 6.7. Standardized Regression Coefficients: Predictors with Social Program Awareness and Program Use, N = 320.

	Social Program Awareness	Social Program Use
Personal Resources		
Political interest	.02	−.02
Political efficacy	.11*	−.05
Internal locus of control	.18***	.07
Life satisfaction	−.04	−.04
Mental health problems	.04	.11
Physical infirmities	−.08	.02
Social Resources		
Rural	−.08	−.06
Group membership	.13	.38****
Social support	−.08	−.11
Age	.07	.01
Education	.00	−.03
Political participation	.05	.01
Married	.14**	−.01
Transportation problems	−.05	.10
Church attendance	−.01	−.02
Male	.17***	.11*
Need (social problems)	−.15	−.14
Program awareness	—	.04
Values		
Individualistic values	.12**	.08
Conservative identification	.08	.09
Multiple R	.43	.40
Multiple R^2	.19	.16
Significance	.0000	.0001

* $P < .10$
** $P < .05$
*** $P < .01$
****$P < .001$

those needs. This is an important finding since research on health care has shown that lack of social support is associated with increased risk for cardiovascular disease, depression, and mortality (Bowling and Brown, 1991).

In the end, these findings may be telling us that we have to better reach out to those with social needs to link them to the appropriate programs. Since these people are outside of existing social networks, though, this will be a difficult goal to achieve. As with nutritional programs, more extensive promotional campaigns and "casefinding" seem called for with rural elderly.

Housing Problems and Policy Implications: An Ecological Approach

The housing environments associated with the elderly have received considerable attention recently. As Robert Bylund (1985) has noted, researchers have looked at the impact in the individual of interior design, intermediate housing, retirement villages, nursing homes, and neighborhood environments. Despite this wide ranging research, conspicuous gaps remain in the literature. For instance, the housing needs of the individual elderly homeowner have been virtually ignored (even though more than 80% of the elderly are homeowners!). This is particularly true with respect to the rural aged; a population that until very recently was seldom studied in the research literature. Indeed, we know very little about their housing needs and its association with their quality of life.

The lack of empirical data on the impact of the housing environment on the quality of life of the rural aged creates a gap in the literature. This is especially significant for the public policy planner as s/he has virtually no information upon which to draw other than intuition in developing housing programs in improving the quality of life of the rural elderly. Yet the importance of the housing environment can hardly be overemphasized.

Montgomery (1972) has clearly stated that housing, an integral part of people's everyday lives, can assume even greater importance for the elderly. He says that (quoted in Bylund, 1985: 38):

The quality of the housing environment becomes increasingly significant in the lives of many aged families and individuals, and the quality of this limited world largely determines the extent to which they will retain their independence; the amount of privacy, auditory and visual, they will experience; how often they will visit friends; their sense of place; and their ability to exercise a measure of control over the immediate environment. Housing is a major variable physically, socially, and psychologically in the lives of older persons.

This takes on even more critical importance when one considers the problems in housing encountered by the aged living in rural areas; these housing problems are often compounded by difficulties in obtaining suitable transportation, distance from medical facilities and hospitals, deficits in physical health and personal skills and abilities, and poverty (Carp, 1976).

We explore the effects of housing on overall quality of life among the rural elderly. In analyzing our data, we place our findings within an ecological framework and propose that a poor housing environment can interact with deficits in sense of personal competence in a vicious downward spiral with no apparently easy avenues of escape.

There have been a number of descriptive ecological models proposed over time (e.g., Lewin's life space model [1951] and Mead's symbolic interactionism [1934], inter alia). Few ecological models have been tested, though, with adult homeowners and fewer still with the elderly.

The one salient exception is the Lawton and Nahemow (1973) ''person/environment congruence model,'' applied extensively to housing environments of the elderly (Lawton, 1980). Researchers maintain that several key factors in the older American's life space can be equally relevant; elements such as the quality of the housing environment of the older person, level of well-being, physical and mental health, and overall life satisfaction—all these factors interact to shape one's overall life satisfaction.

As Lawton (1980) has noted, the interaction of these sets of variables is quite complex and depends upon the fusion of two major clusters of variables conceptualized under the broad categories of environmental press and personal competence. Environmental press (a concept borrowed from Murray, 1938) refers to the demand characteristics of a person's environment such as its quality, its geometric design, spatial relationships with other housing units, and human factors design. In contrast, competence refers to the number of personal resources available to an individual such as biological and emotional health, sensori-motor functioning, cognitive skills, and ego strength (Lawton, 1972).

This interactive model predicts that either increased environmental demands (press) or decreased level of competence will lead to a negative outcome in living as expressed in an individual's behavior, affect, or level of well-being.

A corollary of the person/congruence model is offered in Lawton and Simon's (1968) "environmental docility hypothesis." Specifically, the hypothesis maintains that the less competence an individual has, the greater the negative impact of environmental factors such as inadequate housing.

On the other hand, there is a positive side to this dynamic. For instance, Lawton (1972) suggests that modest improvements in environmental quality might have dramatic effects for a person with major limitations on his or her competence.

More than providing descriptive power, Lawton and Nahemow's theory offers several practical implications to public policy planners for improving the quality of rural elderly homeowners, particularly for those with high personal needs (i.e., with decreased competence) or those with poor quality or otherwise inadequate housing. Recognizing its critical importance, the authors clearly emphasize the point that quality of housing can be directly responsible for a large proportion of an elderly person's decreased life satisfaction.

Thus, inadequate housing and/or decreased competence ought to have a negative impact on the quality of life of the rural elderly. However, good housing and increased competence will have a propitious effect on the quality of life satisfaction of the rural elderly homeowner. Obviously, these people will have fewer problems in their lives and represent the ideal model that we aim to achieve in our recommendations to planners devising social service programs.

Findings. Although 96% of the respondents claimed that they were satisfied or very satisfied with their housing, other data suggest that this sanguine assessment may conceal substantial problems. Briefly, we describe the characteristics of the housing stock and related issues for our sample, based on the 1987 data. The vast majority of respondents are homeowners—81% (very similar to the figure for elderly throughout the nation). 38% of the people claim that their home needs no repairs; 48% claim to need minor repairs; 14% believe that major repairs are in order. 20% say that they set their thermostat at 68 degrees or colder in the winter. This is noteworthy, since cooler homes increase the odds of hypothermia among the elderly, particularly susceptible to this problem. 40% of the homes were constructed in 1900 or earlier; thus, the housing stock is old. While only 4% of the respondents indicate that they are less than satisfied with their housing, 12% contend that they would like to move! 9% indicate that they have trouble paying for utilities. One final item on the questionnaire was an assessment by the interviewer of the state of the respondent's dwelling. 30% of the homes were rated as fair, poor, or extremely poor. Thus, it seems clear that there are greater difficulties than would be gauged simply by the housing satisfaction question.

To better understand what factors are associated with housing problems, we created an overall index representing the extent of housing difficulties. Each person received one "point" for each of the following: saying that the home needs minor or major repairs, having water in the basement often, expressing some dissatisfaction with housing, having problems paying for utilities or rent or mortgage, indicating that the thermostat is set at 65 degrees or less on average, and the interviewer's judgment that the state of repair for the house as fair, poor, or extremely poor. The highest possible score would be 9—indicating very serious housing problems indeed! A score of 0, on the other hand, reflects no problems with housing. The average person has a score of 1. The average older American, then, does not have serious housing problems in Allegany County. Nonetheless, as Table 6.8 summarizes, 15% of the sample has 3 or more problems. Thus, housing poses enough significant problems for Allegany County's elderly that policy planning in this area is in order.

What are the correlates of our index of housing problems? Table 6.9 answers this question. Housing problems are associated with poor nutrition, number of physical infirmities that an individual has, lower education level, greater health problems, more deficits in activities of daily living (ADLs), being younger-old, having less income, having more problems with transportation, having problems paying for things, external locus of control, lower political efficacy, having greater social

Table 6.8. Frequencies: Number of Housing Problems Faced, N = 358.

Number of problems	Frequency	Percentage
0	112	31%
1	121	34
2	73	20
3	34	10
4	15	4
5	3	1
	358	100%

Table 6.9. Pearson's r: Correlates of Housing Problems, N = 358.

	Housing Problems Index
Poor nutrition	.17***
Physical infirmities	.14***
Education	−.18***
Health problems index	.14***
Activities of daily living, deficits	.11***
Age	−.10**
Income	−.18***
Transportation problems	.23***
Problems paying for things	.41***
Internal locus of control	−.20***
Political efficacy	−.15***
Social need	.15***
Group memberships	−.23***
Program awareness	−.12***
Program use	−.08*
Keeps up on public affairs	−.17***
Depression	.11***
Neuroticism	.20***
Life satisfaction	−.24***
Memory problems	.12***
Reduced energy level	.16***

*   P < .10
** P < .05
***P < .01

needs, being isolated from social group memberships, being less apt to keep up with public affairs (i.e., less informed), less aware of public programs and less likely to use them. Finally, housing problems go with greater depression and neuroticism, lower levels of life satisfaction, memory complaints, and lower energy level. All in all, housing problems seem to be part of a complex of negative life experiences with deleterious effects on adjustment and coping.

As previously noted, Lawton and Nahemow contend that the cluster of variables representing housing problems (environmental press) and personal resources (competence) are very important in determining the quality of one's life. To verify and develop appropriate empirically derived variables to reflect press and competence, we conducted a factor analysis. We entered a series of variables that seemed, in one way or another, to tap either press or competence. Table 6.10 reports the results of the analysis.

Factors 1 and 2 seem to represent two different dimensions of .competence. Factor 1 (after Varimax rotation) seems to reflect "biological competence," with poor nutrition, large number of days where illness reduced the ability to carry out normal activities, and deficits in activities of daily living loading most heavily here. The second factor appears to be another competence dimension—this time best labeled as "self-empowerment competence." Internal locus of control, years of education, and sense of political efficacy all load heavily on this factor. Together, these seem to indicate personal empowerment (or personal competence). The final factor clearly reflects environmental press. Loading most heavily on this factor are housing and transportation problems and problems paying various bills. All of these represent environmental demands on the individual that seem to fit the notion of "environmental press."

Next, we test Lawton and Nahemow's critical prediction that the three factors isolated here ought to affect the elderly's quality of life. Table 6.11 presents the results of listwise multiple regression. Only the betas (standardized regression coefficients) appear in this table. The measures of life satisfaction and quality of life that we selected include: having social needs (quality of life goes with fulfillment of social

Table 6.10. Factor Analysis: Environmental Press and Competence, N = 358.

Factors	Problems with Biological Competence	Self-Competence	Environmental Press
	1	*2*	*3*
Housing problems	.07	− .13	.75
Transportation problems	.46	− .06	.50
Poor nutrition	.55	− .09	.17
Internal locus of control	− .44	.62	− .09
Sick days	.64	.10	.09
Deficits in activities of daily living	.69	− .24	− .02
Education	.04	.64	− .31
Political efficacy	.03	.78	− .08
Extroversion	− .34	.41	.06
Problems paying for things	.07	− .11	.81

Table 6.11. Multiple Regression, Standardized Regression Coefficients:
Predicting Quality of Life, N = 351.

	Social Needs	Program Awareness	Program use	Neuroticism	Life satisfaction
Problems with biological competence	.40****	−.19***	.18****	.28****	−.26****
Self-empowerment competence	−.19****	.26****	−.06	−.27****	.22****
Environmental press	.12**	−.20****	.10*	.24****	−.25****
Multiple R	.46	.38	.22	.46	.42
Multiple R²	.20	.14	.05	.21	.18

*   P < .10
**   P < .05
*** P < .01
****P < .001

needs), program awareness and program use (use of programs to meet individuals' needs ought to enhance quality of life), neuroticism (individuals who are consistently depressed and otherwise designated neurotic enjoy life less), and life satisfaction. We use the three factors as predictors of each of these indices of quality of life. In only one case (with program use as dependent variable) does this model fare poorly. With program use, only about 5% of the variance is explained (with a modest multiple correlation of .22). However, the three factors, consistent with Lawton and Nahemow's model, predict the other dependent variables fairly strongly.

Generally, problems in the area of biological competence and environmental press predict greater social needs, less program awareness, fewer programs actually used, more neuroticism, and lower levels of life satisfaction. All of these effects are as anticipated. Au contraire, self-empowerment competence seems to reduce social needs, increase program awareness, diminish neuroticism, and elevate life satisfaction. In each case, the three variables explain a reasonable degree of variance.

Discussion. As anticipated, our findings are consistent with Lawton and Nahemow's person/congruence environment model. Recall that this suggests that personal competence interacts with environmental press to affect quality of life. In general, our findings show that people with high levels of biological competence and self-empowerment tend to face less environmental press and enhanced quality of life. The inverse is true as well.

As Francis Carp (1976) has noted in her extensive review of the housing literature, housing cannot be considered apart from other elements in the environment of the older person. The task is to understand the interplay of environment and the personal characteristics of the resident. As Carp suggests, we report above that housing problems encountered by Allegany County's elderly population are part of a much larger constellation of problems, such as mental and physical health, transportation, nutrition, problems paying for things, and deficits in activities of daily living.

These findings have important implications. For instance, the imply that tackling housing problems of the elderly in isolation from their health problems and other challenges is insufficient. It is apparent that networking and cross-linkage among area human service agencies is the best way to deal with the intertwined multiple needs facing those rural elderly.

We suggest that the communities develop advocacy programs (e.g., see Brown, 1985). These programs would interface with various community service agencies, such as local offices for the aging, the local housing authority, social services, and so on. Such programs would employ an ombudsman who would provide the homeowner with information about the wide spectrum of services available besides home repair and alternate housing. The ombudsman would function as a "broker of services." He or she would provide elderly clients with links to "soft" community services such as meals on wheels, in-home nursing or in-home aide services, health care programs, financial management, psychological or psychiatric services, and the like. The ombudsman and the various service providers could advise clients about the wisdom of moving, about the most appropriate type of facility, and about a myriad services available to the client but about which the older person has no knowledge. As Lawton (1982) has noted, such a program providing neighborhood based support services may make the difference between the person remaining in their home or in becoming institutionalized. The potential cost effectiveness in such a program that maintains people in their homes rather than placing them in institutions is considerable.

Neuroticism, Mental Health, and Policy among the Elderly

Another problem that many elderly confront is depression, neuroticism, and related disorders. This is made more poignant by the simple fact that there is a dearth of psychiatrists and psychologists in rural areas. The need for mental health services for the aged has been well documented. For example, Roybal (1988) reports that between 15% and 25% of the 18 million Americans over the age of 65 suffer from some significant mental health problems. This suggests that as many as 7 million older Americans are in need of assistance. Yet only 4% of patients seen at mental health clinics and 2% by mental health practitioners have been in this age group. This begins to hint at a need-use gap among the elderly.

A number of barriers to the use of mental health services have been identified (Gatz et al., 1985). These include: lack of trained professionals, unwillingness of therapists to treat the elderly, a bias toward the medical model of dispensing medication rather than ''talking'' therapy, the lack of community services for the elderly, and the resistance by many elderly Americans to use extant mental health services.

These barriers are compounded among the rural elderly; federal funding has declined 40% since 1981. Few inpatient services exist within rural counties (only about 13% of these counties have such a service) and only 3% of the psychiatrists nation-wide are employed in rural settings. In addition, there is a traditional reluctance by rural people to use mental health services; access is further limited by lack of transportation. Moreover, it has been found that mental health problems in rural areas tend to be less visible and more geographically dispersed, thus reducing the likelihood of the rural elderly receiving needed services (Healthcare Trends Report, 1990).

Past research has examined the role of social and demographic factors in generating psychological distress. Arling (1987) has examined the relationships between life strain and psychological problems. Social strain has a double-barreled effect—greater stress leads to more mental problems and these, in turn, represent impediments to seeking out counseling services. Those with the greatest needs self-select themselves out of the system!

Revicki and Mitchell (1990) extended Arling's findings to the rural context and discovered a similar pattern. They found that better physical health was highly predictive of life satisfaction and poorer health went with psychological distress among rural elderly. Social strain increased psychosomatic symptoms, although social support mitigated this somewhat.

In Chapter 3, we described the Costa and McCrae NEO Inventory, one component of which was an index of neuroticism. This index included items registering depression as well as other forms of affect disorder. 21% of the respondents had no responses in a direction indicating neuroticism; 31% had three or more and 15% four or more such answers. Despite this, only 5% of the sample (18 persons) claim that they have ever ". . . participated in a support group or had counseling." It appears that there is some gap between need and actual use of counseling services. In the remainder of this section, we explore the correlates of neuroticism; we examine the network of associations which may suggest means of attacking mental dysfunction. Then, we consider those who have at least three responses on the scale in a direction indicating neuroticism; from this group, we compare those who report having used some form of counseling and those who have not been so involved.

Findings. Table 6.12 summarizes the results of multiple regression analysis. A series of social and personal resources and problems facing some older Americans are used as predictors of extent of neuroticism. The Pearson's correlation coefficients show that neuroticism is higher among females, older residents, the less educated, the unmarried, non-homeowners, social isolates, those with housing or social or transportation problems, non-Protestants, people facing nutritional and health problems, and those who report having problems paying bills.

What about the relative impact of each? Listwise multiple regression answers that question. Those variables that emerge as effective predictors of neuroticism (in descending order) include: social needs, health problems, problems paying bills, and fewer group memberships. Thus, it seems that being socially isolated (with concomitant social needs) and facing health and transportation problems may be part of a constellation of situational factors that push people toward depression and other affective disorders. This is common sense, of course.

The last thing that we consider is the difference among those with three or more answers in "neurotic" direction who have had some form of counseling versus those who have had none. The group with which we are dealing here has 107 people. Table 6.13 reports a series of T-tests, to separate out the characteristics of those with some affective dysfunction who use counseling with those who do not. This comparison may suggest something about how to narrow the apparent need-use gap.

Table 6.12. Multiple Regression: Predicting Neuroticism, N = 341.

	Neuroticism	
	r	*Beta*
Male	− .11**	− .03
Age	.09**	− .05
Education	− .24****	− .06
Length of residence	− .03	.05
Married	− .19****	− .04
Homeowner	− .17****	− .07
Group memberships	− .38****	− .16***
Housing problems	.22****	− .01
Transportation problems	.34****	.02
Protestant	− .20****	− .07
Health problems	.39****	.22****
Poor nutrition	.25****	.05
Social needs	.44****	.27****
Problems paying bills	.32****	.19****
Multiple R		.62
Multiple R²		.39
Significance		.0000

*   P < .10
**   P < .05
*** P < .01
****P < .001

For the most part, there seem to be few differences. Among the rare differences to emerge are the following: those who have had some form of counseling are less old, have lived in their current residence fewer years, have more group memberships, are less likely to be homeowners, have fewer health problems, and have modestly better nutrition. Those with some degree of need who do not seek out counseling tend to be the longer term, older, more isolated, and less healthy residents. Since they are isolated, they will be harder to reach out to; outreach programs, then, will be hard put to make contact with this group of people.

Discussion. Our data surely support Arling's findings that social strain has a negative effect on mental health. As Revicki and Mitchell find, we observe that social support (in terms of group involvement) ameliorates psychological distress.

Table 6.13. T-Tests: Among Those with Some Degree of Neuroticism, Comparison of Those Who Have Had Counseling with Those Who Have Not, N = 107.

| | Mean Scores (a) | | | | |
	Counseling	No Counseling	*t*	*df*	*1-tail P*
Male (b)	1.30	1.32	−.12	10.9	.453
Age	71.00	76.16	−2.44	11.6	.016
Education	10.60	10.22	.53	15.1	.303
Years of residence	32.40	50.29	−2.26	14.2	.020
Group memberships	1.80	1.30	1.61	11.7	.067
Social support	2.50	2.36	.58	11.6	.286
Married (c)	.30	.33	−.19	10.9	.428
Homeowner (d)	1.50	1.75	−1.45	10.3	.089
Housing problems	1.50	1.52	−.05	12.5	.482
Church attendance	3.00	3.47	−.77	11.8	.229
Transportation problems	.50	.66	−.67	11.9	.259
Health problems	.50	.97	−1.93	12.6	.039
Poor nutrition	1.10	1.25	−1.35	1.28	.100
Activities of daily living, deficits	.90	1.49	−1.17	13.7	.182
Social needs	.60	.72	−.69	12.4	.253
Conservative ideology (e)	3.10	3.20	−.23	11.2	.412

(a) Separate variance estimates
(b) 1 = female; 2 = male
(c) 0 = no; 1 = yes
(d) 1 = no; 2 = yes
(e) 1 = conservative; 7 = liberal

However, the crucial question remains: Why do so few of the rural elderly with some need for counseling or other related services whom we studied take advantage of extant programs? Our data cannot answer this question, given the limitations that we have already noted (e.g., the lack of variation in the central variable—use of counseling programs). However, previous research points to fewer services simply being available as one problem (Menolascino and Potter, 1989). Some suggest that much more aggressive outreach and promotional efforts are called for in rural areas to ensure that those with all manner of needs receive the proper services (e.g., Young, Goughler, and Larson, 1986; Atkinson and Stuck, 1991; Bender and Hart, 1987).

References

Andersen, Ronald and John F. Newman. 1973. Societal and individual determinants of medical care utilization in the United States. *Milbank Memorial Fund Quarterly* 51: 95–124.

Arling, G. 1987. Strain, social support, and distress in old age. *Journal of Gerontology* 42: 107–113.

Atkinson, Vickie L. and Beverly M. Stuck. 1991. Mental health services for the rural elderly: the SAGE experience. *The Gerontologist* 31: 548–551.

Bear, M. 1990. Social networks and health: impact on returning home after entry into residential care homes. *The Gerontologist* 30: 30–34.

Bender, Carol and J. Patrick Hart. 1987. A model for health promotion for the rural elderly. *The Gerontologist* 27: 139–142.

Berkman, L. F. 1984. Assessing social networks and social support in epidemiologic studies. *Annual Review of Public Health* 5: 413–432.

Botwinick, J. 1984. *Aging and Behavior*, 3rd edition. New York: Springer Publishing.

Bould, S., Sanborn, B., and Reif, L. 1989. *Eighty-Five Plus: The Oldest-Old*. Belmont, CA: Wadsworth.

Bowling, A. and Browne, P. D. 1991. Social networks, health, and emotional well-being among the oldest-old in London. *Journal of Gerontology* 46: S20–32.

Brown, Arnold S. 1985. Grassroots advocacy for the elderly in small rural communities. *The Gerontologist* 25: 417–423.

Brown, Steven D. 1982. The explanation of particularized contacting. *Urban Affairs Quarterly* 18: 217–234.

Bylund, R. A. 1985. Rural housing: perspectives for the aged. In Raymond T. Coward and Gary R. Lee (eds.), *The Elderly in Rural Society*. New York: Springer.

Cahill, K. 1984. Report of the New York State Department Elderly Health Survey. Unpublished report.

Carp, F. M. 1976. Housing and living environments of older people. In Robert H. Binstock and E. Shanas (eds.), *Handbook of Aging and the Social Sciences*. New York: Van Nostrand.

Chernoff, R. 1987. Aging and nutrition. *Nutrition Today* 22: 4–11.

Chernoff. R. and D. A. Lipschitz. 1988. Nutrition and aging. In M. E. Shils and V. R. Young (eds.), *Modern Nutrition in Health and Disease*. Philadelphia: Lea and Febiger.

City Turns . . . 1988. City turns deaf ear to Food Stamp calls. *Comptroller's Report* 13 (February): 1–3.

Clark, M. 1971. Patterns of aging among the elderly poor in the inner city. *The Gerontologist* 11: 58–66.

Cohen, G. D. 1980. Prospects for mental health and aging. In J. Birren and R. B. Sloane (eds.), *Handbook of Mental Health and Aging*. Englewood Cliffs: Prentice-Hall.

Costa, Paul T., Jr. and Robert R. McCrae. 1978. *The NEO Personality Inventory*. Odessa, Florida: Psychological Assessment Resources.

Estes, C. L. and H. E. Freeman. 1976. Strategies of design and research interventions. In Robert H. Binstock and Ethel Shanas (eds.), *Handbook of Aging and the Social Sciences*. New York: Van Nostrand Reinhold.

Frongillo, E. A., Jr., B. S. Rauschenback, D. A. Roe and D. L. Edwards. 1987. *Professional Perspectives*. Ithaca, NY: Cornell University Division of Nutritional Sciences, No. 6.

Gatz, M., Popkin, S. J., Pino, C. D., and VandenBos, G. R. 1985. Psychological intervention with older adults. In J. Birren and K. W. Schaie (eds.), *Handbook of the Psychology of Aging*, 2nd edition. New York: Van Nostrand Reinhold.

Hassen, A. M., N. J. Meima, L. M. Buckspan, B. E. Henderson, T. L. Helbig, and S. H. Zarit. 1978. Correlates of senior center participation. *The Gerontologist* 18: 193.

Healthcare Trends Report. 1990. August. Chevy Chase, Maryland.

Hearings. . . 1969. Hearings before the Select Committee on Nutrition and Needs. U. S. Senate, Part 24, *Nutrition and the Aged*. Washington, D. C.: Government Printing Office.

Human, J. and Wasem, C. 1991. Rural mental health in America. *American Psychologist* 46: 232–239.

Kohrs, M. B. 1986. Effectiveness of nutritional intervention programs for the elderly. In M. L. Hutchinson and H. N. Munro (eds.), *Nutrition and Aging*. San Diego: Academic Press.

Kohrs, M. B., K. Nordstrom, E. L. Plowman, P. O'Hanlon, C. Moore, C. Davis, D. Abrahams, and D. Eklund. 1980. Association of participation in a nutritional program for the elderly with nutritional status. *American Journal of Clinical Nutrition* 33: 2643.

Kohrs, M. B., P. O'Hanlon, and D. Eklund. 1978. Title VII-Nutritional Program for the Elderly. *Journal of the American Dietary Association* 72: 487.

Kovar, M. G. 1977. Health and the elderly and the use of health services. *Public Health Report* 92: 9.

Krout, John A. 1983a. Correlates of service utilization among the rural elderly. *The Gerontologist* 23:500–504.

Krout, John A. 1983b. Knowledge and use of services by the elderly. *International Journal of Aging and Human Development* 17: 153–167.

Krout, John A., Stephen J. Cutler, and Raymond T. Coward. 1990. Correlates of senior center participation: a national analysis. *The Gerontologist* 30: 72–79.

Lawton, M. Powell. 1980. *Environment and Aging*. Belmont: Wadsworth.

Lawton, M. Powell and B. Simon. 1969. The ecology of social relationships in housing for the elderly. *The Gerontologist* 8: 108–115.

Lawton, M. Powell and L. Nahemow. 1973. Ecology and the aging process. In Carl Eisdorfer and M. Powell Lawton (eds.), *The Psychology of Adult Development and Aging*. Washington: American Psychological Association.

Lewin, Kurt. 1951. *Field Theory in Social Science*. New York: Harper and Row.

Maiden, Robert, Thomas A. Leitko, and Steven A. Peterson. 1984. Rural elderly. Presented at Gerontological Society of America, San Antonio, Texas.

Mead, George Herbert. 1934. *Mind, Self, and Society*. Chicago: University of Chicago Press.

Menolascino, Frank J. and Jane F. Potter. 1989. Delivery of services in rural settings to the elderly mentally retarded-mentally ill. *International Journal of Aging and Human Development* 28: 261–275.

Milbrath, Lester W. and M. L. Goel. 1977. *Political Participation*. Chicago: Rand-McNally, 2nd edition.

Moen, Elizabeth. 1978. The reluctance of the elderly to accept services. *Social Problems* 25: 293–303.

Montgomery, J. E. 1972. The housing patterns of older families. *The Family Coordinator* 21: 37–46.

Nelson, Barbara J. 1980. Help-seeking from public authorities. *Policy Sciences* 12: 175–192.

Older Americans. 1971. *Older Americans: Special Handling Required*. Washington, D. C.: National Council on the Aging.

Peterson, Steven A. 1986. Close encounters of the bureaucratic kind. *American Journal of Political Science* 30: 347–356.

Peterson, Steven A. 1987. Older citizens' program encounters. *Journal of Applied Gerontology* 6: 39–52.

Peterson, Steven A. 1988. Stay tuned to your programs. *Journal of Aging Studies* 2: 183–197.

Posner, B. M. 1979. *Nutrition and the Elderly*. Lexington: D. C. Heath Books.

Rawson, I. G., Weinberg, E. I., J. Herold, and J. Holtz. 1978. Nutrition of rural elderly in southwestern Pennsylvania. *The Gerontologist* 18: 24–29.

Revicki, D. and Mitchell, J. P. 1990. Strain, social support, and mental health in rural elderly individuals. *Journal of Gerontology* 45: 267–274.

Roybal, E. R. 1988. Mental health and aging: The need for an expanded federal response. *American Psychologist* 43: 189–194.

Ryan, Alan S., Lisa D. Craig, and Susan C. Finn. 1992. Nutrient intakes and dietary patterns of older Americans: A national study. *Journal of Gerontology* 47: M145–M150.

Sharp, Elaine B. 1982. Citizen-initiated contacting of government officials and socioeconomic status. *American Political Science Review* 76: 109–115.

Smicklas-Wright, H. and G. J. Posmire. 1985. Government nutritional programs for the aged. In R. R. Watson (ed.), *CRC Handbook of Nutrition in the Aged*. Boca Raton, FL: CRC Press.

Snider, Earle L. 1980. Factors influencing health service knowledge among the elderly. *Journal of Health and Social Behavior* 21: 371–377.

Thomas, John Clayton. 1982. Citizen-initiated contacts with government agencies. *American Journal of Political Science* 26: 504–522.

Ward, Russell A. 1977. Services for older people. *Journal of Health and Social Behavior* 18: 61–70.

Ward, Russell A., Susan R. Sherman, and Mark LaGory. 1984. Informal networks and knowledge of services for older persons. *Journal of Gerontology* 39: 216–223.

Weimer, J. P. 1982. The nutritional status of the elderly. *National Food Review* Summer: 7.

Wenger, G. C. 1985. Care in the community: changes in dependency and use of domiciliary services: a longitudinal perspective. *Aging and Society* 5: 143–159.

Young, Christine, Donald H. Goughler, and Pamela J. Larson. 1986. Organizational volunteers for the rural frail elderly. *The Gerontologist* 26: 342–349.

Zuckerman, Alan S. and Darrell M. West. 1985. The political bases of citizen contacting. *American Political Science Review* 79: 117–131.

Chapter 7

Summary and Discussion

It is very difficult to summarize our findings in a few paragraphs. In the preceding chapters, we cover a wide variety of topics, and our results are complex and not always consistent. This is partly due to the purposes of our study. We endeavored to examine the public lives of rural older Americans on three levels. First, we used a broad brush approach examining a wide range of life dimensions and activities. For example, we looked at several dimensions including the political orientations and political participation of the rural aged in relationship to their awareness and use of social service programs.

Second, we considered the program needs of important subpopulations, such as the oldest-old (85 or older), females, and open country/ farm residents. Furthermore, we examined the impact of important specific variables such as personality traits, nutritional needs, quality of health, quality of housing, level of life satisfaction and well-being, and mental health requirements. To organize our study's extensive findings, we applied an overarching five-factor framework modifying somewhat a model introduced by Andersen and his colleagues (e.g., Andersen and Newman, 1973) in which predisposing, enabling, and need factors are defined as primary predictors of program use (see also Andersen et al., 1975). We redefined these and added values and program awareness. This gave us five broad dimensions which included: social resources, personal resources, needs, values, and program-related factors (assessed by program awareness).

We further broke down each broad dimension to subvariables according to the following format: Social resources comprised group memberships, social support, political activism, marriage and place of residence. Personal resources consisted of chronological age, education, personal efficacy, internal locus of control, personality traits,

141

physical health and life satisfaction. Needs measured the problems existing within each specific area (such as nutrition or housing) for a particular group of elderly. Values included a belief in individualism and one's political ideology (conservatism or liberalism). Program-related factors were operationalized as program awareness.

Before we look at our data under the rubric of the aforementioned five factor framework, we first would like to set the stage by briefly describing our rural setting (Allegany County) in which the research was carried out, next outlining our research methodology, and, lastly reviewing our demographic findings.

According to Krout (1986), rural counties are generally distinct from urban communities in that they are characterized by greater poverty, inadequate housing, lack of services, having more inaccessible services, being less likely to participate in informal and formal organizations, and being predominantly white.

Allegany County is no exception. It is a fairly large county, sparsely populated, and located in the Southern Tier of Western New York. It comprises 670,000 acres, about a third of which is used for marginal agricultural and dairy farming. Its population is relatively small, 51,860 people of whom 8211 (16%) are elderly. The median income is one of the lowest in the state. The dominant industry is farming although about one in five individuals is employed in heavy manufacturing. Politically, the county epitomizes conservative values and is predominantly Republican. Thus, in many ways Allegany County is indistinguishable from and typical of the vast majority of rural counties (Krout, 1986). Indeed Allegany County appears to be the quintessence of rural America.

In 1983 and 1987, we sent throughout this rural county trained interviewers to survey the needs and program use of a random sample of older Americans. They administered an amended form of the well validated Older Americans' Status and Needs Questionnaire (Brukhardt and Lewis, 1975). All told (counting respondents in both 1983 and 1987), our interviewers contacted 1053 people, of whom 814 agreed to be interviewed. This represents a 77% response rate, quite good by survey standards. To insure that people from all parts of the county and from the population centers would be included, we stratified our population by town size and by location (the northern versus southern half of the county).

Summary of Demographics

The samples revealed the following descriptive demographic characteristics. The average age of our respondents was 74 years old; about

44% lived alone. About 64% were female and 36% male. Almost everyone was Caucasian (99%), 44% were married and 55% had at least a high school education. Approximately 89% said they were satisfied with their lives. Most were in fairly good health. About 72% were judged without an infirmity and 28% percent had at least one, with 14% having two or more. However, we ought to note that despite these rather positive findings mentioned above, the respondents manifested numerous problems. About 26% claimed to have one or more problems with transportation. Around 32% said they have more than one social need; 69% asserted they have one or more housing problems. Poor nutrition was faced by a small but substantial 15% of the sample. While most said (88%) they had enough money, an ample minority (21%) said they had problems paying for important items such as prescription drugs, food, heating and medical bills. Although most of our sample appeared to be mentally healthy, about 20% indicated they were either depressed or emotionally distressed. Yet only 5% had received any formal counseling. The median income was only $7000 as compared to the national average of $10,000 to 14,000 (NORC data, 1987)—and one of the lowest in the state of New York. About 35% were below the poverty line with another 44% seemingly in marginal circumstances. Less than 7% had incomes of $18,000 and above in 1987. One must admire the "courage" of the county's elderly to maintain a positive outlook in the face of rather bleak objective circumstances. One very positive note, though, is that the elderly faced a low crime rate; fewer than 3% reported any contact with crime.

The Five Factor Model

Although most researchers of rural needs recognize that we can no longer continue to employ single variable or two factor models in attempting to understand and explain awareness and use of social service programming (Krout, 1986), very few studies utilize a multimodal approach. Most have implemented single or dual factor models in attempting to understand and to explain awareness and use of social service programs. We developed a multifaceted model as a more comprehensive method to organize the data. Our model examined the combined impact of social resources, personal resources, need, values and program-related factors on program use.

Analyses. We begin our analyses by looking at the impact that the social resources factor had on program use. It seems logical that one's social being affects program use. However, the exact impact of social resources is not well understood in the literature. The research is mixed (Havir, 1991; Andersen, 1968). Sometimes having good social resources has been cast as a facilitator of program use, sometimes as an inhibitor. We found that group ties and social support predicted greater program use, while being married and being male predicted less use. Social support also went with increased political interest and willingness to use mental health services. Being low in social resources was particularly important. We found that low levels of social resources were associated with lack of political interest or public affairs, more housing problems, greater nutritional needs, more rural residence, being male, less educated, and less churchgoing. The socially isolated were less likely to make use of nutritional programs designed to meet their needs such as meals-on-wheels. And the oldest-old were the most socially needy among the elderly, while they were generally the least likely to use social programs designed to address their needs.

In general, then, social resources was an important dimension. We found modest but significant correlations suggesting that people low on social resources tended to have a high need for services even though they were less likely to participate in social service programs, whereas people high on social resources tended to express greater use of social programs even though they had less documented need for them.

Next, we look at the impact of our second factor, personal resources, on program use. In the case of personal resources, we see a similar set of predictions as was suggested for social resources. For example, it can be argued that older people who possess many personal resources ought to have less need for services and, therefore, use them less than those who have fewer personal resources. Or reminiscent of the rich get richer phenomenon, we might expect people high on personal resources to actually participate more in governmental programming even though their need is lower.

However, we found at the most global level that the dimension of personal resources was uncorrelated with program use. When we decomposed the dimension, we found that a number of variables were correlated with program use. For example, we found that poor physical health and poor mental health were correlated with greater nutritional need and greater nutritional program use. And, we found those elderly high on personal resources but who had problems in housing were more likely to use county social service programs than those low in personal resources. This makes good sense as we expect resourceful people to take advantage of available services to help render their problems manageable. We also discovered, to digress slightly, that those elderly high in personal resources felt more in control of their lives, more self-empowered, and more self-reliant.

Next, we look at the sub-dimension of personal resources: personality traits and its impact on program use. In many ways, one can liken personality to an intervening or moderating variable in determining program use. It stands between social and personal resources and need for services. The elderly person's personality traits can be likened to a consistent and stable decision-making mechanism that facilitates or hinders the use of social service programming. For example, the elderly who scored high on the traits of openness and extroversion were likely to be political active and to be in control of their lives and to have less need and use of services.

But personality can cut two ways. For example, people high on the trait of neuroticism (about 15%) tended to be less politically active and to be in greater need of nutritional, mental health and housing services. However, their utilization of such services was disappointingly low. Although a host of other problems may be associated with neuroticism, it seems clear that this personality trait of neuroticism interfered, to some degree, with the use of social service programs.

We also found that the most rural elderly (those living in the country/ farm versus in the village) tended to be less open, more traditional and set in their ways, less tolerant of others and generally more rigid. They also tended to be younger and healthier and matched the stereotype of the rugged individualist. For the most part, they as a group tended to have a low need for social service programming.

Next, we consider a factor related to personality traits: an older person's value system. We frequently read about the rugged individualism and self-reliance of the rural elderly. The rural elderly (and for that matter we believe this fact is true for most elderly regardless of where they live) prefer not to be dependent on others, including close family members. They want to be independent and to live on their own for as long as they can manage or get away with it.

Many researchers contend that the putative conservative values and the attitudes of the elderly are responsible for their reputed resistance to using governmental sponsored programs and are a major constraint limiting the effectiveness of the delivery of these services (See Calsyn, 1989).

However, we found this not to be the case as the values and the attitudes of the rural elderly were for the most part uncorrelated with the use of programs. However, we did find one exception to this pattern. People high on individualistic values were more likely to take part in congregate meal programs. This may suggest that our rural elderly can be conservative in terms of their beliefs and values, but pragmatic in terms of their actions such as taking the opportunity occasionally to enjoy an inexpensive and prepared meal on the county.

The fourth factor we consider is need. Again, the now familiar pattern of the literature prevails: It is mixed. Some researchers insist that having abundant social and personal resources are the most important in predicting service utilization by the elderly (See George, 1981). Others argue that unmet need is the most important dimension, explaining the largest proportion of the variance in service use (See Krout, 1986).

In general, we found the latter not to be the case. Sadly, and counterintuitively, and in contradiction to the declared goals of many governmental programs for the aged, we found that those elderly with the most need generally evinced little or modest use of available social programs devised to meet their needs. Our findings suggested a curvilinear relationship (Also see Krout, 1983): the youngest-old and the oldest-old tended to use programs the least while the middle-aged (or old-old, if you will) tended to use programs the most. This was true even though they had little or no need for the programs as they were by and large quite a healthy and active segment of our elderly rural population. Indeed the people who demonstrated the most need for programs—the impoverished, isolated, and female—tended to fall into the oldest age category and were least likely to participate in social programs.

This last finding underscores the general pattern of program use we have consistently found throughout our study: The most needy people fail to take full advantage of governmental programs, while the less needy, most often, do. This conclusion is disturbing and ought to concern public policy makers and program planners.

Finally, we investigate the fifth dimension: program-related factors or program awareness on program use. Program awareness has been held by several researchers as the fundamental factor affecting service utilization (See Krout, 1986). Thus, we expected to find a strong association between program awareness and program use. Much to our surprise, program awareness was only modestly related to program use and only in the instance of our 1983 sample. This may be partially explained by the facts that many programs such as congregate meals were well known and advertised and elderly tended to use only one or two services, lowering the variance of our data. Yet, it seems eminently logical that one is generally aware of a program first before he/she subscribes to it. However, others have reported similar findings (See Fowler, 1970 for a discussion). We are unsure how to interpret this finding. Although it appears as though program awareness is less important in program use than is generally believed, we still contend that it is an important component in the path to receiving needed services. Efforts should be made by outreach workers to inform the rural elderly of the various services that are available to them.

Conclusions. Our findings can be seen as partially supporting a multidimensional model (as originally proposed by Andersen *et al.*, 1975). Social and personal resources and predisposing factors such as program awareness were significantly related to program use albeit they explained only a modest proportion of the variance of program use. However, for the most part, unmet need and values were not. This latter finding is certainly one of the critical findings of our study from an humanistic point of view as it underscores the shortcomings of governmental sponsored programs as they are currently constituted in rural areas. Indeed with such modest correlations it almost seems that utilization of governmental programming is just as subject to chance factors as to the intentions of its designers.

Discussion

Obviously, more research needs to be done to tease out the various specific and interactive contributions of the factors outlined above on program use. However, the basic conclusion remains: public programs are not working very well in terms of addressing the needs of the most needy rural aged. Why?

We believe that part of the answer lies in the way services are delivered in rural areas. Social planners tend to address the needs of the elderly on a unitary basis. They target specific areas of concern and develop single programs to address that need. For example, the area of nutritional need is addressed by congregate meals. And oftentimes more than one program is developed to meet a similar need. For example, there are congregate meal programs, meals-on-wheels programs, and food stamps. But often these programs address the same need. Yet, they are administered in a hodge-podge fashion frequently with little attention other than lip service given to interfacing or coordination among the various programs. Administrators often ignore the reality that the needy rural elderly tend to live in multiple jeopardy and have multiple needs. We believe that what is needed is the designing and implementation of multimodal programs that address a wide variety of elderly needs in one fell swoop.

We are not the first authors to discover problems in who utilizes programs. Bernice Neugarten pointed out over a decade ago (1980) that very frequently the elderly who had the least need for services were the most likely to use them. And those who had the greatest need for services—the poor, the disabled, and the isolated—were the least likely.

However, her proposal for a solution was somewhat different than ours. She challenged the use of entitlement programs that are simply based on chronological age rather than being based on need. She argued for an "age irrelevant society." She maintained that in an era of federal budget deficits and of budget trimmers, social service programs for the elderly should be based on need (not age), the way many other social services operate, e.g. food stamps and Medicaid.

We do not totally embrace her ideas on this point for the following reason. It is possible that social service programs for the elderly may serve a positive and ameliorating function even if they are not always being utilized by the dire needy. For example, participation in such programs by the healthy elderly may help keep them active and involved in their communities. In this way, participation serves as a protective buffer. It can forestall senility and early debilitation that may have fallen upon them had they not capitalized on these programs. Indeed, numerous studies have shown that the use of available social networks by the elderly functions as a protective barrier helping them preserve their health and independence, reduce social isolation, increase morale and well-being, and delay the onset of institutionalization right up to the last minute (Havir, 1991) where the elderly person may simply fall apart as in Oliver Wendell Holmes' allegorical story "The Wonderful 'One-Hoss Shay' " (Quoted in Schaie and Geitwitz, 1982).

Furthermore, we speculate that it is possible that once these otherwise healthy rural elderly utilize governmental programs, they ought to develop the habit of continuing to use them even as they age and presumably develop more need for them.

Certainly this possibility needs to be considered more extensively. To do so would require longitudinal research. What happens to these middle-aged old program users as they get older? As they grow older and frailer, will they plummet out of the social service nexus (like ancient sky divers whose parachutes have failed them)? Or will they remain protected by the social service network until the very end? We simply do not have the data to even begin to answer this very important question.

Until this research is performed, we find ourselves with the following nagging but essentially humanistic question: How do we get people with unmet need to use services more?

Multimodal approaches. To this end, we suggest that agencies and other providers of services for the elderly pool their resources to provide a "package of affiliated services" to address the multiple needs of the impaired and otherwise disadvantaged elderly. Many authors have suggested this approach and Lawton (1985) had good success in an early demonstration project. His project provided a group of highly impaired elderly with "a package of services" directed by a case manager. They received in-home help such as a homemaker, home health care, and home delivered meals. These services enabled them to live longer in their own homes rather than having to be placed in a nursing home.

Besides the obvious direct impact of the program, the package of services aided the highly impaired recipients in enhancing their control over their decreased life-space. Their favorite living room chair became their centerpiece from which they monitored the front door, the street through their window, the telephone, the television set, and—in most cases—the radio. Many had lavatory facilities placed nearby. Like an ancient baron or baroness of a small principality, they possessed full control over their modest life-space. The extension of control over a decreasing living area plus the array of in-home services positively affected the overall life satisfaction and subjective well-being of the recipients.

Our findings clearly demonstrate that a multimodal approach is required. Single program approaches are not very effective and leave too much up to chance factors and happenstance. We found that many complex factors are involved in the use of social service programs— such as social factors, personality traits, personal resources, possibly motivating attitudes and values, unmet need, and program awareness.

Indeed, governments are increasingly aware of the need for such coordinated action. New York State's EISEP (Extended In-Home Services for the Elderly) program, for instance, uses case managers to try to coordinate addressing the different unmet needs of poor, frail elderly in order to allow them to remain in their own homes. Additionally, such a program is expected to save government money by keeping such people out of nursing homes which would cost much more.

Census targeting. We suggest that these programs ought to begin by identifying the most needy through sophisticated manipulation of available Census data. We have shown in the body of our work that impairments tend to cluster with a host of other deficits. Population densities with the designated cluster of deficient characteristics could be targeted. And advocacy outreach workers could be sent to these areas to contact these elderly and address the multiple needs.

How would this work? Respondents of similar demographic characteristics tend to cluster or live in the same neighborhood and community. For instance, it has long been known in Allegany County that the oldest-old are found in much higher numbers in certain communities. A perceptive service provider could take advantage of this by targeting those special areas for outreach programs to boost the number of people contacted in a cost-efficient manner. The elderly in such communities can be interviewed regarding their unmet needs, informed of services available to help them, and referred (voluntarily) to the appropriate agency(-ies). Targeting communities this way is a very efficient method of getting the "word" out.

Furthermore, "cross-referencing" census data further rationalizes the process. One could analyze the data looking for cluster densities by combining multiple traits such as poor housing features, transportation problems, nutritional deficits, and low income. Targeting individuals in these communities for special attention would further help agencies productively contact those people more likely to have multiple needs.

Empowerment needs. However, simply offering services to the rural elderly is not enough. This could foster increased feelings of dependency and cause the elderly to perceive themselves as less in control of their lives (Rodin and Langer, 1977; Langer, 1983). The approach taken ought to be proactive. Offered programming must be packaged in such a way that it enhances the rural citizen's perception of internal self-control and self-empowerment and decreases the perception of being out of control or developing feelings of learned helplessness (Berkowitz, Waxman, and Yaffe, 1988; Lawton, 1990; Seligman, 1975; Maiden, 1987). It has been shown that the mindful enactment of perceived control over behavior yields positive psychological and physical consequences with elderly populations that may significantly increase their psychological well-being (Langer, 1983). Thus, it is essential that every step possible be taken to insure that the elderly are active and willing participants of any governmental program devised for them.

Additional thoughts on outreach. Outreach, aggressive and focused, can be a useful mechanism to generate greater linkage between unmet needs and program usage. One model, targeting elderly who needed mental health services, emphasized the following: reducing the stigma attached to using certain types of programs, by ensuring that the program's name was neutral sounding; outreach personnel must build extensive networks within the community, in order to begin to get referrals from community agencies and informal groups and leaders (including pharmacists, grocers, and so on) who have extensive contact with the elderly (Atkinson and Stuck, 1991). To facilitate outreach, developing a cadre of volunteers is important. Older Americans with an interest in taking part and church and youth organizations are likely candidates to get involved. Those willing to participate did the following: (a) draw up an inventory, from their own knowledge, of elderly in need of services; (b) professional staff and volunteers went to the homes of the target elderly to carry out needs assessment and intake; (c) services were provided where appropriate (Young, Goughler, and Larson, 1986).

Promotional campaigns can be useful, too. One example: Articles were placed in local papers and public service announcements on radio stations to make older Americans more aware of health issues and the services provided by a health clinic in rural Oklahoma. Notices went to senior citizens' groups, including nutritional and recreational programs (Bender and Hart, 1987). That such efforts work is exemplified by the finding that use of at least some programs is enhanced greatly as the service becomes more visible to the community (Hayslip, Ritter, Oltman, and McDonnell, 1980).

Although our findings are modest and frequently explain only a small proportion of the variance of program use, they do demonstrate that, no matter how well-intentioned the delivery of social services to the elderly, needs are not being optimally met within existing community structures that coordinate programs within rural communities, although many improvements have been made in the process in recent years (e.g., Alter, 1988). It is clear that the needy aged ought to be turning to and receiving services—whether from government or other sources—more often. As usual, more research, especially longitudinal research, needs to be done.

However, we offer some caution. Our research is based on cross-sectional findings which are necessarily limited and tell us little about cause. While this type of research may be a first step in describing the statistically significant correlations of program use and in underscoring the potential problems, we believe rural researchers have reached the limits of such designs. What is needed are new longitudinal designs and panel analyses. This type of understanding (Havir, 1991) may be particularly germane to rural elderly who have generally demonstrated greater needs for governmental programs yet possess fewer personal resources and lack the alternative services frequently found in the more resource rich urban counties.

References

Alter, Catherine Foster. 1988. The changing structure of elderly service delivery systems. *The Gerontologist* 28: 91–98.

Andersen, R., J. Kravits, and O. W. Andersen. 1975. *Equality in Health Services*. Cambridge, MA: Ballinger.

Andersen, Ronald and John F. Newman. 1973. Societal and individual determinants of medical care utilization in the United States. *Milbank Memorial Fund Quarterly* 51:95–124.

Atkinson, Vickie L. and Beverly M. Stuck. 1991. Mental health services for the rural elderly: the SAGE experience. *The Gerontologist* 31: 548–551.

Bender, Carol and J. Patrick Hart. 1987. A model for health promotion for the rural elderly. *The Gerontologist* 27: 139–142.

Berkowitz, M., R. Waxman, and L. Yaffe. 1988. The effects of a residential self-help model on control, social involvement, and self-esteem among the elderly. *The Gerontologist* 28: 621–624.

Brukhardt, J. E. and J. C. Lewis. 1975. *The Older Americans' Status and Needs Assessment Questionnaire*. Washington, D. C.: Department of Health, Education, and Welfare.

Calsyn, R. J. 1989. Evaluation of an outreach program aimed at increasing service utilization by the rural elderly. *Journal of Gerontological Social Work* 14: 127–135.

Costa, Paul T., Jr. and Robert McCrae. 1985. *The NEO Personality Inventory*. Odessa, FL: Psychological Assessment Resources.

Fowler, F. J., Jr. 1970. Knowledge, need and use of service among the aged. In C. C. Osterkind (ed.), *Health Care Services for the Aged*. Gainesville, FL: Institute of Gerontology, University of Florida.

George, Linda K. 1981. Predicting service utilization among the elderly. Paper presented at Gerontological Society of America meeting.

Havir, L. 1991. Senior centers in rural communities: potentials for serving. *Journal of Aging Studies* 5: 359–374.

Hayslip, Bert, Jr., Mary Lou Ritter, Ruth M. Oltman, and Connie McDonnell. 1980. Home care services and the rural elderly. *The Gerontologist* 20: 192–199.

Krout, John A. 1986. *The Aged in Rural America*. Greenwich, CT: Greenwood Press.

Krout, John A. 1983. Correlates of senior center utilization. *Research on Aging* 7: 455–471.

Langer, E. J. 1983. *The Psychology of Control*. Beverly Hills: Sage Publications.

Lawton, M. Powell. 1985. The elderly in context: perspectives from environmental psychology and gerontology. *Environment and Behavior* 17: 501–519.

Maiden, Robert J. 1987. Learned helplessness and depression. *Journal of Gerontology* 42: 60–64.

Neugarten, Bernice. 1980. Acting one's age: new rules for old. Interviewed by Elizabeth Hall. In Harold Cox (ed.), *Aging*. Guilford, CT: The Dushkin Publishing Group.

Peterson, Steven A. 1987. Older citizens' program encounters. *Journal of Applied Gerontology* 6: 39–52.

Rodin, J. and E. J. Langer. 1977. Long-term effects of a control-relevant intervention with the institutionalized aged. *Journal of Personality and Social Psychology* 35: 897–902.

Schaie, K. Warner and James Geitwitz. 1982. *Adult Development and Aging*. Boston: Little, Brown.

Seligman, M. E. P. 1975. *Helplessness: On Depression, Development and Death*. San Francisco: Freeman.

Young, Christine, Donald H. Goughler, and Pamela J. Larson. 1986. Organizational volunteers for the rural frail elderly. *The Gerontologist* 26: 342–349.

Name Index

Subject Index